THE MORE TIME MOMS

PROJECT PLANNER

EDITIONS
More Time Moms
PUBLISHING INC.

GRAPHIC DESIGN BY
Sorin Pavelesco

ILLUSTRATIONS BY
Albert Prisner

DESKTOP BY
Dan Sokolowski

PHOTOGRAPHY BY
Hélène Anne Fortin

EDITED BY
Joanne Lalonde-Hayes • Patricia Lalonde

SPECIAL THANKS TO THE MOMS AND DADS WHO WROTE THIS BOOK

CONTRIBUTING AUTHORS:
Robert Bourassa • Marlene Daly • Marie Dumais
Lise Durand • Lorna Gregoire-Gauthier • Jeremy Hayes
Joanne Lalonde-Hayes • Patricia Lalonde • Claude Leblanc
Grant Lugg • Cathy Nolan • Carole Presseault • Teresa Stanley

COPYEDIT/PROOFREAD BY
Danielle Lalonde • Marla Fletcher

PRINTED IN CANADA BY
Friesens Printers

EDITIONS

More Time Moms

PUBLISHING INC.

HELPING YOU PUT YOUR FAMILY FIRST

Our mission is to create, produce and market tools to make your life easier so you can spend more time with your family.

THANK YOU PARENTS FOR YOUR TERRIFIC FEEDBACK ON LITTLE HELPER

Our great adventure to produce the ultimate planner for moms continues. Special thanks to the moms and dads who used the first edition of Little Helper and who have taken the time to share their suggestions and improvements. A big thanks as well to our tester-moms who never fail to call it as they see it. Your contributions have helped create this system and we hope it helps you.

Please let us know how we can help in the future and how we can improve our products to better serve you. Please feel free to contact us with any questions regarding this, or any of our other products.

TO REACH US:
More Time Moms Publishing Inc.
PO Box 455, Aylmer, QC, Canada J9H 5B7
Tel: 819-684-0046 • Fax: 819-684-9197
email: mtmoms@istar.ca
internet site: www.moretimemoms.com

TABLE OF

MANAGING THE HOUSEHOLD

TAKING CARE OF THE FAMILY

CONTENTS

GETTING AWAY

SPECIAL PROJECTS

Dear Parents,

The More Time Moms Little Helper and Project Planner are designed to work together.

Little Helper, is for managing your time, your bills and for housing the paperwork you will want to keep with you when you are out of the house. The monthly calendars are undated so that you can begin using Little Helper at anytime.

The Project Planner is where to keep the information relevant to your projects. Use it like a workbook. Cross things out, check things off, tear sheets out at will. There is no one way to use this book and we're going to make you a new one next year, so make this one work for you now. The planner is straightforward and simple to use but I should explain two things before you begin. You will notice that some pages are laid out with more than one check box so that you can use the list several times. If you plan to use these pages more than once, then use the left most check box the first time around. Once you have finished with the list just toss it into your back cover pocket until the next time. You will also see some lists with a line over-top a column of check boxes. This is so because these lists are for more than one person. Place the initial of each person over one of the columns of check boxes.

A note of caution before you begin; this is not a "make work" system. We are trying to help you spend more time with your families, not less. This planner is not meant to add to your "I have to's." It is meant to be fun and easy and to help you with the things that you "want to do", so please use it this way.

We sure hope you like it and we are looking forward to hearing from you.

Cheers,

Joanne

MANAGING THE HOUSEHOLD

AAAH, WOULDN'T LIFE BE GRAND IF WE HAD OUR OWN CHEFS? Most of us don't, but many of us have a husband and children. Now, if we had a plan that could deliver us amazing family meals and use the resources we have at our disposal, then we wouldn't need a chef so badly. The best way to reduce most of the work and stress involved with feeding your family is to delegate what you can and prepare weekly menus & grocery lists. Read through this section and build your menus and grocery lists in Little Helper. Start with one week, see how it goes. You can use it as as a backup when things get chaotic or, if you like the whole concept, you can plan a couple more weeks and then just rotate them.

TO-DO LIST!

- [ ] Get your family members to list their favourite meals.
- [ ] Delegate some of the work.
- [ ] Build your menus and grocery lists in Little Helper.

CHILDREN CAN MAKE THEIR OWN BREAKFASTS, SNACKS AND SCHOOL LUNCHES at a surprisingly early age. Most 10-year-olds can do a good job. All you need to do is to keep on hand, foods that are good for them and that they like to eat. As a bonus you can put an end to the uneaten lunch dilemma because they won't pack it if they don't like it.

WHAT ELSE CAN YOUR FAMILY MEMBERS DO? If you refer to the chores for kids section in this book you will see a listing of kids chores. Refer to the ones that have to do with meals and see if you can delegate some more of the work.

▼ MEALTIME CHORES	▼ WHO AND WHEN

KIDS "MAKE YOUR OWN"

Check off the foods your children like best and keep a combination of these foods on hand at all times so your children can prepare their own breakfasts, snacks and lunches.

- ☐ Cold cereal
- ☐ Milk, juice
- ☐ Fruit
- ☐ Bread, rolls
- ☐ Bagels, croissants
- ☐ Biscuits, crackers
- ☐ Muffins
- ☐ English muffins
- ☐ Pita bread, crisps
- ☐ ....
- ☐ ....

- ☐ Tortilla shells
- ☐ Corn chips
- ☐ Popcorn
- ☐ Cleaned veggies
- ☐ Seeds and nuts
- ☐ Dried fruit
- ☐ Peanut butter
- ☐ Honey, jam
- ☐ Marmalade
- ☐ ....
- ☐ ....

- ☐ Cream cheese
- ☐ Cheese
- ☐ Cold meats
- ☐ Egg, tuna salad
- ☐ Chicken salad
- ☐ Hummus
- ☐ Salad dressing
- ☐ Dips, salsa
- ☐ Yogurt
- ☐ ....
- ☐ ....

INCLUDE LOTS OF FRUITS AND VEGETABLES IN YOUR CHILDREN'S DIET. For easy to use vegetables, wash and store them in air-tight containers. You can even make your own pre-made salads by throwing in all kinds of veggies including brocoli, cauliflower, string beans, etc. Make a jar of dressing for the week and voilà! Salads to go that even the kids can make for their lunches.

FAMILY FAVOURITES

Use the space on the next page to record your family's favourite meals. Once complete, post it on your fridge. It will help you out at 6:00 pm, when you are staring blankly in front of the freezer wondering what to make for dinner, until you have built your menus and grocery lists.

BREAKFAST
Bacon and eggs
Eggs Benedict
Omelet
Quiche Lorraine
French Toast
Pancakes
Crepes
Waffles
Hot cereal

LUNCH, SNACKS
Soup, hot or cold
Salads, Coleslaw
Sandwiches
Pizza
Nachos
Leftovers
Veggies and dip

PASTAS AND SAUCES
Bolognese, Marinara
Alfredo, Carbonara,
Pesto, Primavera
Oil, garlic & Parmesan
Lasagna
Cannelloni
Manicotti

SALADS
Garden
Caesar
Greek
Pasta
Three Bean
Broccoli

ROASTED/BAKED
Beef
Chicken
Ham
Pork
Pork tenderloin
Fish, Salmon
Lamb
Shell fish

MORE SALADS
Cobb
Leafy
Niçoise
Chicken Caesar
Main course

KIDS LIKE 'EM
Brochettes
Burritos
Chicken fingers
Chicken pot pie
Chili
Fajitas, Tacos
Fish Fillets
Hamburgers
Macaroni & cheese
Pizza
Shepherd's pie
Sloppy Joe's
Spaghetti
Spareribs
Stew
Hardy soup
Stir fries
Stuffed Potatoes

▼ OUR FAVOURITE MEALS

MEAL	WHERE'S THE RECIPE?

CHORES FOR KIDS

WHY DELEGATE CHORES TO YOUR CHILDREN? It is important to delegate chores to your children so that you have help at home and so that they can learn to take care of themselves. Contributing to the family in this fashion will teach your children self-discipline, enhance their self-esteem and build a sense of pride through achievement. Please remember that chores are not meant to be a punishment and we don't want our children to view them as such.

SHOULD YOU PAY FOR CHORES? We believe that the work children do in the home should be classified in two groups, chores and jobs. Each family member should contribute to taking care of his person and to the household duties on a regular basis without pay. We call these tasks chores. Children will learn that adults do a lot of things in life without pay and that their contribution to the home is expected. Chores should include daily and weekly tasks with an emphasis on taking care of oneself and one's things. Jobs, on the other hand, are different. Children need to learn how to seek employment, negotiate wages, have an opportunity to earn pocket money and learn to manage money. What better place to learn these skills than at home? Jobs at home can include any tasks not already delegated as chores, along with seasonal and project tasks. You can assign dollar values to jobs and let your children choose their work, or better yet, you can teach your children initiative and job hunting skills by letting them look for work around the house that needs to be done and, if it will be helpful to you, you can pay them for it.

START EARLY. It comes very naturally for children to want to help out at a young age and we must not discourage it. Even a two-year-old can put napkins on the table for dinner, but if you have never asked your 14-year-old to do chores, trying to get her to put napkins on the table for dinner will be an ordeal.

ASSIGN BOTH DAILY AND WEEKLY CHORES. Your children's chores should include daily tasks, such as putting away their things as they use them and setting the table. Save weekends for the bigger jobs such as cleaning their rooms and other rooms in the house.

CHORES

START BY HAVING THE CHILDREN TAKE CARE OF THEMSELVES: When assigning chores to your children, start with those that involve taking care of his or her own self. Like anything in life, we must learn to be independent before we can become interdependent, and it is much easier for children to do things for themselves than for others.

COACH YOUR CHILDREN THROUGH THEIR CHORES: It may seem time- consuming at first, but every time a child takes on a new chore he needs to be trained and supervised before he can undertake it alone. Make your expectations clear and take the time to show your child the way you would like things done and the way it should look when he is finished. You may have to stay with your child two or three times before he gets it right and can do it on his own, but the time you spend coaching him will be time well spent.

BE GENEROUS WITH YOUR PRAISE: Your children are not going to be able to complete their chores the way you would for quite some time. Do not complain about their efforts. Be patient and praise your children often for their contributions.

HOMEWORK COMES FIRST: Make sure your child takes care of his or her schoolwork before all other chores. Most children do best by taking care of their homework right after school. A snack, a chat and then into the homework helps set the pace for the rest of the evening, as well. It clears the way for family discussion time at dinner and a relaxing evening that eases into bedtime.

ROTATE YOUR CHILDREN'S CHORES. Rotating your children's chores will go a long way to avoiding the boredom and complacency that can occur if children have to do the same thing over and over again. Record the children's schedule on your Family Organizer or other spot on your communications board.

DELEGATE YOUR FAMILY CHORES: Take a minute to delegate some household chores. Remember: Whatever you don't delegate, you will end up doing yourself.

HELPER	CHORES	NEW CHORE	HELPER	CHORES	NEW CHORE

You cannot expect your toddler to have the same tasks as your teenager. The blue chores are chores that you can delegate to a toddler. A 13-year-old should be able to do every chore on this list. When complete, post this master chore list somewhere handy for all to see. If your child has bathroom duty this week as his weekly chore, he or she can refer to his column to see exactly what is expected. Place one child's initials above a column of boxes and check off each chore that he is to do. Increase your children's responsibilities as they grow.

DAILY CHORES

- Make beds
- Put away toys, books
- Put away music, tapes
- Put clothes in hamper
- Put away own things
- Make own breakfast
- Make own lunch
- Help prepare dinner
- Set the table
- Serve dinner
- Make coffee, tea
- Serve dessert

- Clear the table
- Wash dishes
- Dry dishes
- Fill dishwasher
- Empty dishwasher
- Wipe kitchen surfaces
- Sweep the floor
- Take out trash, recycling
- Pick up mail
- Feed pets
- Exercise pets

OUTSIDE CHORES

- Take trash to roadside
- Take recycling to roadside
- Tidy yard
- Tidy deck
- Weed gardens
- Water planters, gardens
- Water lawn
- Mow lawn
- Trim lawn
- Maintain pool

- Vacuum pool
- Sweep driveway
- Shovel driveway
- Shovel walkway
- Tidy shed
- Tidy garage
- Clean out car(s)
- Vacuum, dust car(s)
- Wash outside of car(s)

WEEKLY CHORES AND OCCASIONAL CHORES

▼ BEDROOMS

- ☐☐☐☐☐ Dust
- ☐☐☐☐☐ Put away clean clothes
- ☐☐☐☐☐ Tidy desk
- ☐☐☐☐☐ Tidy shelves
- ☐☐☐☐☐ Tidy closets
- ☐☐☐☐☐ Tidy drawers
- ☐☐☐☐☐ Clean, vacuum floors
- ☐☐☐☐☐ Change sheets
- ☐☐☐☐☐ Empty trash
- ☐☐☐☐☐ ....
- ☐☐☐☐☐ ....
- ☐☐☐☐☐ ....

▼ BATHROOMS

- ☐☐☐☐☐ Clean tub
- ☐☐☐☐☐ Clean sink, counters
- ☐☐☐☐☐ Clean toilet
- ☐☐☐☐☐ Clean mirrors
- ☐☐☐☐☐ Clean floors
- ☐☐☐☐☐ Tidy cabinets
- ☐☐☐☐☐ Tidy shelves
- ☐☐☐☐☐ Change towels
- ☐☐☐☐☐ Check toilet paper
- ☐☐☐☐☐ Empty trash
- ☐☐☐☐☐ ....
- ☐☐☐☐☐ ....

▼ KITCHEN

- ☐☐☐☐☐ Wash the floor
- ☐☐☐☐☐ Wipe cabinets
- ☐☐☐☐☐ Wipe down fridge door
- ☐☐☐☐☐ Clean out fridge
- ☐☐☐☐☐ Wipe down chairs
- ☐☐☐☐☐ Help plan menus
- ☐☐☐☐☐ Prepare grocery list
- ☐☐☐☐☐ Do groceries
- ☐☐☐☐☐ Unpack groceries
- ☐☐☐☐☐ Cook meals
- ☐☐☐☐☐ ....

▼ COMMON ROOMS

- ☐☐☐☐☐ Dust furniture, pictures
- ☐☐☐☐☐ Dust and tidy shelves
- ☐☐☐☐☐ Clean mirrors
- ☐☐☐☐☐ Clean TV screen, stereo
- ☐☐☐☐☐ Vacuum couches
- ☐☐☐☐☐ Vacuum rugs
- ☐☐☐☐☐ Clean floors
- ☐☐☐☐☐ Empty trash, recycling
- ☐☐☐☐☐ ....
- ☐☐☐☐☐ ....
- ☐☐☐☐☐ ....

▼ HOUSEHOLD

- ☐☐☐☐☐ Do own laundry
- ☐☐☐☐☐ Sort family laundry
- ☐☐☐☐☐ Fold own laundry
- ☐☐☐☐☐ Clean pet cages
- ☐☐☐☐☐ Bathe and groom pets
- ☐☐☐☐☐ Water plants
- ☐☐☐☐☐ ....

MOM'S WEEKDAY ROUTINE

Schedule your regular household jobs here. Taking the time to plan out your weekday routine will save you time and ensure things get done.

MONDAY	TUESDAY	WEDNESDAY	THURSDAY	FRIDAY	SATURDAY
MORNING					AM
AFTER WORK					PM
AFTER DINNER					EVENING

▼ SPRING INTO ACTION

Spring cleaning. It's a chore and it's a bore! But schedule it in; either plan to spend a whole weekend on it or do one room a night for the week. Whatever the plan, enlist the help of family members, turn up the music, roll up your sleeves and go to it. When the job is done, reward everyone with a meal out. Arm yourself with a minimum of tools and carry them around with you for maximum efficiency. You will need:

- sponges, rags
- rubber gloves
- bucket, mop
- broom, vacuum
- toilet brush
- old toothbrushes
- trash bags
- stepstool or ladder
- paper towels
- all-purpose cleaner
- tub and tile cleanser
- ammonia
- abrasive cleanser
- chlorine bleach
- window cleaner
- white vinegar

▼ SPRING CLEANING CHECKLIST

▼ KITCHEN

- [ ] Clean refrigerator inside and out; vacuum coils and underneath
- [ ] Clean out kitchen cabinets, drawers
- [ ] Clean oven, exhaust fan and hood
- [ ] Wash out garbage can
- [ ] Scrub kitchen floor
- [ ] Wipe cabinets
- [ ]
- [ ]

▼ BATHROOM

- [ ] Change or wash shower curtain, liner
- [ ] Clean shower doors and bath mat
- [ ] Scour tile grout
- [ ] Clean out medicine cabinet
- [ ] Discard expired drugs, prescriptions
- [ ] Clean out drawers, cabinets
- [ ] Clean behind toilet
- [ ] Scrub floor
- [ ]

▼ AROUND THE HOUSE

- [ ] Wash walls, switches, doorknobs
- [ ] Vacuum baseboards, window sills, heating vents
- [ ] Vacuum bookcases, picture frames, lampshades
- [ ] Vacuum under furniture
- [ ] Polish, oil or wax furniture
- [ ] Spot clean or clean upholstery
- [ ] Shampoo carpets and rugs
- [ ] Clean wood floors
- [ ] Clean mirrors, light fixtures
- [ ] Clean blades on ceiling fans
- [ ] Clean out fireplace
- [ ] Wash windows, blinds
- [ ] Change and clean window dressings
- [ ]
- [ ] Rotate, flip and vacuum mattresses
- [ ] Reorganize linen closet
- [ ] Launder, air out blankets, comforters
- [ ] Sort, clean winter clothing for donation and storage
- [ ] Change or clean a/c filters
- [ ] Change furnace filter
- [ ] Drain sediment from hot water heater
- [ ] Safety check, p 18
- [ ]
- [ ]
- [ ]
- [ ]
- [ ]
- [ ]

▼ OUTDOORS

- ☐ Clean and repair outdoor furniture
- ☐ Inspect roof for leaks, broken and missing shingles
- ☐ Clean out gutters, drainpipes
- ☐ Inspect house exterior for repairs
- ☐ Inspect grounds for repairs
- ☐ Scrape, prime, paint peeling spots on trim or woodwork
- ☐ Clean out barbecue
- ☐ Check fences, steps and pathways for repair
- ☐ Scrub wooden decks and treat with wood sealer or paint
- ☐ Service lawn mower and sprinkler system
- ☐ Reactivate outdoor faucets, hook up and test hoses
- ☐ ....

▼ FALL CLEANING CHECKLIST

INDOORS

- ☐ Clean fireplace
- ☐ Inspect chimney
- ☐ Inspect & tune up furnace
- ☐ Clear and clean registers and grills
- ☐ Inspect water heater tank pressure
- ☐ Inspect temperature relief valve
- ☐ Insulate water pipes, unheated areas
- ☐ Insulate attic floors
- ☐ Seal air leaks around windows
- ☐ Install plastic sheets on windows
- ☐ Safety check, p 18
- ☐ ....

OUTDOORS

- ☐ Inspect the roof
- ☐ Clean out gutters, drainpipes
- ☐ Check storm drains for debris
- ☐ Caulk cracks, windows, door frames
- ☐ Check exterior doors for tight seals
- ☐ Replace worn weatherstripping
- ☐ Check foundation for cracks, termites
- ☐ Store outdoor furniture, flowerpots
- ☐ Close down pool
- ☐ Shut off outdoor water, sprinklers
- ☐ ....
- ☐ ....

CLEAN GREEN	SOLUTIONS
Countertops, cupboards, walls	Dish soap, baking soda, warm water
Floors	2 T vinegar, 1 cup water
Windows, mirrors	2 T borax, 3 cups water Polish with newspaper
Mildew	Apply vinegar & salt paste
Carpet spot cleaner	Blot with mixture of vinegar & soapy water
Carpet freshener	Sprinkle baking soda or cornstarch & vacuum
Furniture polish	1/2 C lemon juice to 1 C olive oil
Bathroom cleanser	1/2 C vinegar to 2 cups water
Drain cleaner	1C baking soda + 1 C vinegar Let react for 15 mins. Flush with hot water.
Stain remover	Baking soda & lemon juice
Air freshener	Simmer cinnamon, orange peel & cloves.

A FIREPROOF HOME

Don't be under the false perception that fire will never happen in your house. There's a 1-in-10 chance of a fire at home. Major causes of residential fires are: smoking, deep friers, frayed electrical cords, electrical shorts and overloads, space heaters and stoves.

AN OUNCE OF PREVENTION

- ☐ Install smoke detectors and carbon monoxide detectors
  Min: one per floor or one outside every bedroom.
- ☐ Keep fire extinguishers in handy locations, out of children's reach.
- ☐ Create a fire safety plan.
- ☐ Teach your family what to do in case of fire.

THE GREAT ESCAPE PLAN

Get your family together and draw a floor plan of your home. Have each family member sketch out his/her room. Your escape plan should show:

- ☐ Two ways out of every room
- ☐ At least one smoke alarm per floor
- ☐ Local fire department phone #
- ☐ An outdoor family meeting place

Have routine fire drills and practice different scenarios. Pretend smoke is blocking the doorway or blanketing the room. Use a stopwatch to time your escapes.

BEDTIME FIRE SAFETY ROUTINE

- ☐ Unplug all electrical appliances
- ☐ Check if cigarettes still burning
- ☐ Empty ashtrays (contents are cold)
- ☐ Close guard on fireplace
- ☐ Switch off portable heaters
- ☐ Close doors of unoccupied rooms

SIX MONTH SAFETY CHECK

- Replace smoke alarm & carbon monoxide detector batteries
- Vacuum detector units
- Check flashlight batteries
- Pressure gauges on fire extinguishers
- Inspect & correct for hazards
- Practice your home fire escape plan

IN CASE OF FIRE

1. Don't panic.
2. Don't ever stay inside. Don't hide.
3. If there's smoke, stay low and crawl.
4. Get out quickly, closing doors between you and the fire.
5. Test doors by looking, listening and feeling before opening.
6. Once you're out, call the fire department from a neighbor's or phone booth.
7. Stay out. Never go back into a burning building.
8. If your clothes catch on fire, STOP, DROP and ROLL!

* For additional information, fire safety advice and literature, contact your local fire department or the National Fire Prevention Association (NFPA).

A WELL-RUN HOME

Did you know that the average person loses 29 minutes a day just looking for paperwork that is on his/her desk? Now can you imagine how much time you spend walking over clutter, moving clutter, cleaning clutter and searching for items like keys and sunglasses. Reorganizing your home so it works for you is a project that you are going to want to do eventually. Not today perhaps, and definitely not all at once, but sometime — for this a super time-saving project. Even if your home works well for you now, this section offers some good ideas.

It's Easy! This section is laid out in sub-projects so that you can tackle your house one room at a time. In general, all you need to do is:

- Determine the use, purpose and activity for the room
- Rid the room of all superfluous furniture and clutter; cleaning as you go
- Reorganize the room and furnishings to suit the use and support the activities in the room
- Find a place for everything you are keeping, taking time to find a permanent home for the time-wasters we can never find: keys, sunglasses, purses, etc.

Start each room by sorting clutter with zest, eliminating everything you can. You will need basic cleaning supplies, a garbage bag and three cartons labeled:

- GIVE AWAY: It is easier to get rid of things if you know they are going to someone who could use them. Take these boxes out to the car when you are done, so that you can dispose of them on your next trip. Consider having a garage sale or selling these items to a consignment store.

- STORE AWAY: Designate a storage area in your home and create an easy storage system using cartons and shelving units. Get new cartons, uniform in size and that fit onto your storage shelving unit. Clearly label the boxes in general categories such as Christmas, Children's Artwork, Camping Supplies, etc., and bring them to the storage area when they are full.

- SOMEWHERE ELSE: The items in this box belong to another room in the house.

CAUTION! Do not nag or force everyone in the house into this project. Do your children's rooms with them and be respectful of their choices and their possessions. If your spouse is not interested in participating, move and work around his/her things and do not throw out his/her stuff.

▾ ENTRANCEWAYS

- ☐☐ Use your cartons to clear out old, broken, seldom-used and unnecessary iter from these rooms. Clean as you go and store out-of-season clothes elsewhe if you are short on space.
- ☐☐ Organize the closet and furnishings to suit your needs. Make sure your childr can easily get to and put away their things. If you have a back or si entrance, customize it for them.
- ☐☐ Give each of the following items a permanent home. Assign drawers or shelv in the entranceway for each family member's personal items.

Keys	Purse, wallet	Shoes, boots
Sunglasses	Briefcases	Hats, scarves, gloves
Pocket items	School, sport bags	Umbrellas

▾ MAIL SYSTEM

The best way to close the floodgates on incoming clutter is right here, in one of your entrance ways. To establish a system for your mail and other incoming paper you will need:

- ☐ A place inside the house to leave mail so everyone can pick up their own; Choose a basket, bowl or tray big enough to house packages and newspapers. Instruct the children to leave their school paperwork in here too. If your spouse prefers to empty mail more slowly than you, you can get him/her a personal basket.
- ☐ A place to put the mail to keep, answer or store; preferably a spot in your office for mail that needs your attention, a storage box for each child, in his/her room or in your storage area for school records and artwork that you want to keep.
- ☐ A place to put newspapers and magazines to be read; set up by your reading area to house current reading material only.
- ☐ A place to record information from mail you are not going to keep; use your Family Organizer or calendar to record dates or current information regarding the household and children.
- ☐ A recycling bin for envelopes and mail you won't keep.
- ☐ A place for outgoing mail, parcels and the like.

LIVING ROOM AND FAMILY ROOM

- [ ] Before you begin uncluttering and organizing, you must decide what kinds of activities will take place in each room. It will help to think in areas rather than rooms for this project.

READING AREA

- [ ] Comfortable seating
- [ ] Good lighting
- [ ] Books, newspapers, etc.
- [ ] Place for eyeglasses
- [ ] ....

CONVERSATION AREA

- [ ] Comfortable seating
- [ ] Low lighting
- [ ] Surface for drinks, etc.
- [ ] ....
- [ ] ....

MUSIC AREA

- [ ] Stereo equipment
- [ ] Low lighting
- [ ] CDs, cassettes, tapes
- [ ] Place for instruments
- [ ] ....

GAMES AREA

- [ ] Place to store games, puzzles and cards
- [ ] Table
- [ ] Chairs
- [ ] Lighting over table
- [ ] ....
- [ ] ....

PLAY AREA

- [ ] Lots of room
- [ ] Good lighting
- [ ] Place for toys *(use bins, baskets to sort toys, books)*
- [ ] ....
- [ ] ....

TV AREA

- [ ] Television equipment
- [ ] Remote controls
- [ ] TV listings
- [ ] Videotapes
- [ ] Video camera
- [ ] ....
- [ ] ....

- [ ] Clear out and sort the items using your cartons. Clean as you go and make sure to remove all items and furnishings that do not belong. Clear out broken, unused and dated things, keeping only the latest newspapers, magazines and catalogs. Make a trip to the library to donate books that have become clutter. Remove all dust collectors such as knick-knacks and souvenirs that seem to gather in these rooms.

- [ ] Arrange the furniture and lighting to set the right atmosphere for each area, and find a permanent home for items within each area.

THINGS I NEED TO BETTER ORGANIZE THESE ROOMS

- [ ] ....
- [ ] ....
- [ ] ....
- [ ] ....
- [ ] ....
- [ ] ....
- [ ] ....
- [ ] ....

▾ KITCHEN

☐ Clear out and sort your kitchen items using your carton system. Be ruthless a try to keep your countertops as clear as possible. Here is an easy guide.

— If you haven't used it in a year, give it away or throw it out.
— If you use it every couple of months, store it in the storage room.
— Every month, store it in an out-of-the-way cupboard.
— Every couple of days, store it in a handy cupboard or drawer.
— Every day, leave it on your counter.

☐ Set up your kitchen in work stations to minimize traffic, maximize efficiency. Keep the things you need handy to each work station.

▼ COOKING, STOVE

- Pots, pans, oven mitts
- Cooking spices, oils
- Cooking utensils
- Baking soda

▼ FOOD PREP

- Utensils
- Cutting board, knives
- Lunch bags, containers
- Canned, dry food
- ....
- ....

▼ SINK

- Dish soap, hand soap
- Dishwasher detergent
- Vegetable peeler, brush
- Colander, cutting board
- Dishrags, towels, etc.
- Trash container, bags
- Recycling containers

▼ DISHWASHER

- Utensils
- Glasses, dishes
- Napkins, placemats

▼ MIXING, BAKING

- Bowls, casseroles
- Cookbooks, recipes
- Cookie sheets
- Baking pans
- Measuring spoons
- Measuring cups
- Mixing spoons
- Spatulas, mixer
- Blender, processor

▾ COMMAND CENTRAL COMMUNICATIONS SYSTEM

Every home needs a place to keep track of the family's comings and goings, appointment messages, etc. If you keep your More Time Moms Family Organizer on your bulletin boar along with the following items, you will have an instant communications station. Bonus Now you will know where to find a pen when you need one.

Calendar	Pens, pencils, erasers	Bulletin board, tacks
Telephone	Paper	Trash container
Telephone books	Surface to write on	Scissors
....	....	....

BATHROOM & LAUNDRY ROOM

- [ ] Start by getting rid of old cosmetics, medications, cleaners and all clutter and dirt. Leave very little on countertops, sinks and tubs. Clean as you go.

- [ ] Reorganize your bathrooms and find a permanent home for even the smallest of items. Remember to keep medications and cleaners out of children's reach. Here's a good idea: if your space is limited, prepare a basket for each child containing his/her own personal grooming supplies. He/she can keep in his/her room when not in use.

▾LAUNDRY SYSTEM

- [ ] Remove clutter and clean as you would any other room.

- [ ] Set up a place for pocket items, clothes to be mended, clothes to be hand-washed, clothes to be ironed, darks, coloureds and whites.

- [ ] Take a few minutes before you start to think about who could help with which parts of the laundry, and when they could do it. Include the children in these duties and arrange your dirty and clean laundry basket placement either in your laundry room or other rooms throughout the house to facilitate the work.

▼ LAUNDRY CHORES	▼ WHO AND WHEN
Put the laundry into hamper	
Bring it to laundry room	
Sort the laundry	
Wash and dry the laundry	
Fold or hang the laundry	
Put away the laundry	
Iron the laundry	
Put away iron	
Mend clothes that need mending	
Take clothes to dry cleaner	
Pick up clothes from dry cleaner	

▼ THINGS I NEED TO PICK UP TO BETTER ORGANIZE THESE ROOMS

- [ ] ....
- [ ] ....
- [ ] ....
- [ ] ....
- [ ] ....
- [ ] ....

▾ CHILDREN'S BEDROOMS

☐☐☐☐ To begin, sit down with your children and list the activities that wil take place in their bedrooms. It's their space and they should have a say i everything, including the colour of the walls. The more your children can clai ownership of their rooms, the more likely that they will enjoy and clean them.

....

....

....

....

....

....

☐☐☐☐ Sort through the room using your boxes. Clean as you go.

☐☐☐☐ Organize the furniture and items in these rooms so your children ca access everything in the room and easily manage his/her chores. Place the be away from the wall, customize the closet to your child's height and belongings, us boxes or drawers under the bed, keep things handy to where they will be used an keep it simple. Carpets and stuffed animals are great dust collectors. Remov carpeting and place all but your child's favorite stuffed animal on a shelf, particularly if your child has respiratory problems. Provide lots of floor space fo playing and a well-set-up workspace for homework.

☐☐☐☐ Find a place for the clutterers. In a small child's room you can use bins, buckets or baskets to sort books and toys. Store the bins on shelves, unde the bed or in the closet. This way, your child can take down a bin when she/he wants it, carry it around, play with the toys and then easily return the bin to its proper place.

▼ THINGS I NEED TO PICK UP TO BETTER ORGANIZE THESE ROOMS

☐	☐ ....
☐	☐ ....
☐	☐ ....
☐	☐ ....
☐	☐ ....

▾ MASTER BEDROOM

e master bedroom is our special — and sometimes only — retreat. The atmosphere re should be especially comfortable and pleasing. It is much easier to relax in an derly and harmoniously decorated room than an overcrowded one.

Clear out all your clothes, one space at a time. Start with your smallest dresser and work your way up to the closet. Put your clothes in one big pile and clean out the dresser or closet.

Sort clothing using the cartons. Ship out everything you can. If you haven't worn it this year, what makes you think you will wear it next year? And about that skinny wardrobe you are hanging onto, the chances of you being thin at the same time that your wardrobe is back in style are pretty remote. Besides, if you do get skinny again, you are going to want to treat yourself to new clothes. Give it away. Old purses, shoes and accessories? Give them away. Store seasonal items and things you don't use regularly. Throw out torn, worn and broken items and take everything that doesn't belong in your room out.

Now look at the clothing you have left and decide where you want to keep it. Be logical in your choice and do not overpack drawers, shelves or closets. Consider your closet and what it will house. There is a lot of unused space in most closets. Customize your closet to your needs. Do you need extra shelving, racks for shoes, extra rods, boxes for accessories? If you have done a good job sorting, you will be surprised at how much room you now have.

Go through the rest of your room and find a place for everything. Look for interesting containers to house your things in — trunks, armoires, under-bed drawers, baskets, etc. Separate little things in small containers instead of throwing everything into larger containers.

THINGS I NEED TO BETTER ORGANIZE THIS ROOM

- [ ] .... ☐ ....
- [ ] .... ☐ ....
- [ ] .... ☐ ....
- [ ] .... ☐ ....
- [ ] .... ☐ ....

▼ HOME OFFICE

- [ ] Start by clearing out the old, the broken, the unused and outdated items. Take the tim go through all the paperwork in your office, throwing out and cleaning as you go.
- [ ] Organize your workspace so your supplies are close at hand and remember to find a pl for everything, right down to your paperclips. Use small trays or plastic baskets to s small items in your drawers. The more dividers you put in your drawers, the less tim will take to find things.
- [ ] Store original important paperwork in a safe; use duplicates for your files.
- [ ] Scheduling a specific time every week for office work can keep the time spent on it t minimum.

▼ BASIC HOUSEHOLD FILING SYSTEM

The key to a well-run office is to establish a system for managing your incoming an outgoing paperwork. Here is a basic household filing system. The first five files ar holding files, files that you move paperwork through. Once paperwork has moved throug the holding files, it is filed in the current files. When those files become outdated or n longer necessary you can move them into storage files or into the trash. You are going t want to customize your filing system, so feel free to add other files. An expandable fi folder is a simple and inexpensive way to organize your current files.

▼ HOLDING

- [ ] Mail
- [ ] To do
- [ ] To file
- [ ] Bills to pay
- [ ] Things pending

▼ CURRENT

- [ ] Banking
- [ ] Utilities
- [ ] Medical
- [ ] Income stubs
- [ ] Purchase receipts

▼ STORAGE

- [ ] Income tax
- [ ] Insurance
- [ ] Mortgage
- [ ] Wills
- [ ] Children
- [ ] Original documents

▼ THINGS I NEED TO BETTER ORGANIZE THIS ROOM

It's easy and it's important: Making your money work for you is easier than it looks, and you can make it quite enjoyable. Set aside one evening a month for you and your spouse to share a bottle of wine, your dreams, your future and your financial progress.

You must understand your financial situation before you can begin financial planning. Start by filling in the cash-flow budget on the next page. Setting up your budget will enable you to assess your disposable income, direct your savings, reduce your debt, eliminate the stress associated with your finances and enhance your peace of mind.

- The first thing you need to do is determine the net after-tax income that comes into your home. Include all household income.

- Next, record your monthly expenses in the "actual" column. Some of these numbers are easy to pin down, your mortgage or rent for instance. Some are yearly or weekly expenses such as municipal taxes or groceries, that you will need to break out on a monthly basis. Other expenses, such as clothing may require some time before you can determine them. You may need to review your expenses over the last year or, if you are without records, you can record your expenses for a month or two before beginning your budget. Either way, it is critical to determine all your expenses before building your budget.

- Once you have laid out your expenses, you will be able to see exactly where your money is going and where you might be able to reduce your expenses. Use the budget column to set your objectives for the coming year. Some expenses cannot be reduced in the short run, such as mortgage payments, but others may be ripe for reduction. Your budget objective should be to reduce expenses wherever possible in order to create more disposable income. Once you have gone through this process, you will be amazed at how significant a few simple changes can be to the overall financial health of your household. Use the last column to make notes to yourself.

CAUTION! A budget is only as good as it is realistic. Your budget must suit your needs and add quality to your life, not stress. Do not set your budget expenses so low that they are unachievable, otherwise you will get discouraged and abandon the process. Start by reducing expenses that seem wasteful and will not cause undue hardship for family members. Start slowly and learn to live within your budget before you set more aggressive objectives.

BUDGETING

MONTHLY NET INCOME	ACTUAL	BUDGET	COMMENTS
Salary			
Other Income			
Total Net Income			

MONTHLY EXPENSES	ACTUAL	BUDGET	COMMENTS
Mortgage/Rent/Condo Fees			
Municipal Taxes			
Home Insurance			
Utilities			
Phone - Fax/Internet/Cell/etc.			
Groceries			
Dining Out			
Auto Insurance			
Auto - Gas/Repairs/Plates/etc.			
Other Transportation			
Loans/Credit Cards			
Interest/Service Charges			
Savings Fund			
Children's Education Fund			
Life Insurance			
Health Insurance			
Medical/Dental			
Child Care			
Clothing/Shoes			
Sports/Activities			
Entertainment			
Vacation Fund			
Gifts/Donations			
Club Memberships			
Newspapers/Subscriptions			
Total Expenses			
DISPOSABLE INCOME			

▾ KEEPING TRACK

An easy way to keep track of your expenses is to purchase twelve 8.5 by 11 inch envelopes and label them January through December. If you can find the ones that have expense forms printed on them great, if not, layout 12 sheets of paper, either by hand or on your computer like the one below and staple one to the front of each envelope.

DATE	STORE	ITEM	AMOUNT SPENT

Remember to keep all your receipts. This may take a while before it becomes automatic for you, but carry on, until it does. Once a week, empty your wallet of receipts, throw them into the appropriate envelope and record them on the front of the envelope. This is the simplest way to collect the data you need for a proper budget, to monitor your expenses and to retrieve receipts for returns.

OR: Some of our customers have modified the pages in Little Helper to keep track of their expenses. If you would like to do the same, just use the running to do lists and layout a table at the top of the page similar to the one above. You will still need a place for your receipts, but all your info will be handy to you in your Little Helper.

▾ MANAGING YOUR CASH THE OLD FASHION WAY

If money flows through your fingers like water and you really want to stick to your budget, you may just have to do it the old fashion way. Allot yourself a certain amount walking-around money per month. Take that money out in cash and put it into 4 envelopes. At the beginning of each week, take the money from one of the envelopes and put it into your purse. And that's it, that's all you can spend that week, or month if you run over. Do not take more money from the bank, if it's gone, you'll just have to wait until next month.

▼ MY FIVE-YEAR PLAN

Take the time to define your objectives for the future. Remember the wine, get settled and then ask yourselves the following questions: Where do we want to be in five years, in 10 years and in 20 years? Consider your lifestyle, your dreams, your children's education, your mortgage, your finances and your retirement plan when answering these questions. Be as explicit as you can when setting your long-term goals.

▼ MY MONTHLY CASH FLOW IS NEGATIVE

The first order of business on the road to financial health is to be debt-free. In order to pay down debt quickly and efficiently, begin by listing your debts below. Your strategy should be to pay the minimum monthly amount on all debt and in addition, put as much down per month as possible on the debt with the highest interest rate, typically credit cards, until that debt is paid off. Once that debt is cleared, continue with the same strategy until all debt is paid.

▼ I'LL PAY OFF THESE DEBTS:	BY: MM/YY	INT. RATE	MONTHLY PAYMENT
☐			
☐			
☐			
☐			
☐			

HOME INSURANCE

Home insurance is meant to protect us from loss in case of theft, fire, flood and other acts of nature. More often than not people are underinsured and, in case of disaster, find themselves unable to replace their belongings. Use the following form to list the contents of your home. Doing this exercise will not only help you estimate the amount of insurance coverage you need for your home, it can act as an inventory for the contents of your home in case of tragedy. Keep this form safe from fire along with pictures and receipts of your valuables, to settle claims quickly and fully. Without good records, insurance companies will have a harder time assessing the real value of the claim and it could take a long time to settle.

MY HOUSEHOLD INVENTORY

EXPENSIVE ITEMS	ACTUAL VALUE	REPLACEMENT VALUE
Jewelry, silver		
China, crystal		
Works of art		
Computer equip.		
Television equip.		
Camera equip.		
Stereo equip.		
Musical instrmts.		
Large appliances		
Bikes		
Sports equip.		
Outdoor equip.		
Clothing, men		
Clothing, women		
Clothing, children		
Machinery		
Tools		
TOTAL:		

MY HOUSEHOLD INVENTORY

FURNISHINGS	ACTUAL VALUE	REPLACEMENT VALUE
Living room		
Dining room		
Family room		
Kitchen		
Bedroom #1		
Bedroom #2		
Bedroom #3		
Bedroom #4		
Bedroom #5		
Home office		
Bathrooms		
Laundry room		
Basement		
Garage		
Storage room		
Porch, patio		
TOTAL:		
TOTAL PAGE 31:		
GRAND TOTAL:		

TAKING CARE OF THE FAMILY

Getting ready for Back to School can be hectic if you are not organized, but a few minutes of planning can make the transition smooth and easy. There are just a couple of things to do: make some arrangements, buy a lot of stuff and lay out a typical school day routine. Use the next two pages to take care of the to-dos and the to-buys. You can tear out these lists and keep them in your purse or your car, so you can take advantage of the Back to School sales. Now that that's taken care of, you need only sit down with your children and build your School Days Routine. Once complete, tear the schedule from your planner and post it somewhere for easy reference.

School Days Routine: We strongly recommend you and your family work out before and after school routines to clarify responsibilities and avoid upsets on school days. Children perform best within a structured environment, and avoiding chaos and panic on school days is essential to your sanity and to their well-being. Use the schedule in this section to lay out their routine and consider these points as you go: (1) Homework: Make sure the children have quiet and well-lit places to do their homework and keep their school books. Schedule homework time when it best suits your child. Some children do best with a snack and half an hour outdoors before doing their homework. Check your children's homework regularly. (2) Designate chore times for both the children's daily and weekly chores. Chores for Kids follows this section; refer to it when filling out your school days routine. (3) Think about the things that cause upset in the household for the kids and find a solution to avoid these upsets. If your daughter gets frantic in the morning because her jeans are not clean, perhaps it's time for her to learn how to do her own laundry. (4) Children should do some physical activity and have some outdoor time every day. (5) Lay out your routine with your family to make sure everyone's needs are considered, and that everyone is contributing to the family and to household duties.

A Great Adventure! Encourage your children to view school as a great adventure and loads of fun. Children take their cues from their parents and if we worry, are apathetic or show separation anxiety, they will have a harder time settling in, especially at first.

An Ounce of Prevention! Walk the safest school route with your small children to either the bus or the school before class begins. Give them specific instructions as to where to walk and cross, how to handle strangers and what to do or not do. Prepare and practice emergency routines with your children, in case they leave school early or you are delayed.

TO DO

- Arrange after-school care
- Verify school bus schedule
- Arrange emergency alternatives
- Sort through kids' clothes
- Mend or alter clothing
- Label supplies, clothing

TO BUY

- Clothing
- School supplies
- Medicines
- Extra house keys
- Bus tickets, passes
- Locks for bikes, lockers

FOR SCHOOL

CLOTHING

- Underwear
- Socks, stockings
- Shirts, blouses
- Pants, jeans
- Skirts, dresses
- Sweaters, jackets
- Indoor shoes
- Outdoor shoes
- Uniform

GYM BAG

- Shorts, T-shirt
- Sneakers
- Swimsuit, towel
- Bathing cap, goggles

OUTDOORS

- Raincoat, umbrella, boots
- Winter coats, snowsuits
- Winter boots
- Hats, scarves, mittens, gloves

WE NEED TO PICK UP.....

CONSOLIDATED SCHOOL SUPPLY LIST

Use this page to consolidate your children's school supply list.
Tear it out and keep it with you to take advantage of back to school sales.

HOW MANY?	ITEM	HOW MANY?	ITEM

KIDS' SCHOOL DAYS ROUTINE

MONDAY	TUESDAY	WEDNESDAY	THURSDAY	FRIDAY	SATURDAY
BEFORE SCHOOL					AM
AFTER SCHOOL					PM
AFTER DINNER					EVENING

The best way to ensure your family's health care needs are met is to establish a good relationship with your health care provider. Your family physician, pediatrician or nurse can provide you and your family the right information to make decisions about your health.

WHAT TO EXPECT

- Someone supportive.
- Someone you feel comfortable with. You shouldn't feel intimidated.
- Someone who is available to you when you need them and who can help you with backup arrangements when they are away.
- Someone who understands your needs.

▼ CHECKLIST FOR CHOOSING A HEALTH CARE PROVIDER

- [ ] Ask family and friends, neighbors and co-workers.
- [ ] Telephone local faculty of health sciences or professional associations for referrals.
- [ ] Is the office far away? Are the hours convenient?
- [ ] Consider your first visit a tryout.
- [ ] Come prepared. Make a list of your symptoms, things you want to talk about.
- [ ] Are you comfortable with the physician, dentist or nurse? Did you know that poor communication can lead to misdiagnosis?

WHEN DO YOU SEE THE EYE DOCTOR?

Poor eyesight has been linked to poor learning. Optometrists suggest infants and toddlers have their first eye examination at the age of six months. Preschool children should have an examination at the age of three and prior to entering schools. Children between six and 19 should have their eyes examined annually.

KEEPING YOUR TEETH AND GUMS HEALTHY

- Caring for your baby's gums is as easy as wiping the gums with a washcloth or sterile gauze at least once a day.
- Brush & floss at least twice a day.
- Eat sensibly. To encourage the development of healthy teeth, pregnant moms should eat a healthy, balanced diet that is rich in calcium.
- Visit your dentist twice a year. Baby's first visit to the dentist should be between the ages of one and two.

WHAT TO DO AFTER HOURS

Emergency rooms and walk-in clinics are not always the best place to receive the care you need when you need it. Talk to your health care provider about what you should do in emergency situations. You should see a doctor if your baby is under six months of age and has a fever, or if your child has a temperature over 39°C (102°F).

GETTING READY FOR LIFE'S EMERGENCIES

Remember to fill out and post your emergency information sheet, in Little Helper.

▼ FAMILY MEDICINE CHEST*

- ☐ Prescriptions, medicines
- ☐ Pain and fever relief
- ☐ Acetaminophen — do not give ASA or aspirin to children unless prescribed
- ☐ Thermometer
- ☐ Medicine spoon, oral liquid syringe
- ☐ Ipecac syrup to induce vomiting — call your local poison center before using
- ☐ Sunscreen — 15 SPF or higher
- ☐ DM — dextromethorphan — dry cough
- ☐ Petroleum jelly
- ☐ Diaper rash ointment — zinc
- ☐ Saline nose drops
- ☐ Calamine lotion
- ☐ Rubbing alcohol — to clean tweezers and thermometers
- ☐ Cotton swabs and balls
- ☐ Tweezers, small nail clippers
- ☐ First aid kit
- ☐ ....
- ☐ ....

* as recommended by the Canadian Pharmacists Association

▼ FAMILY FIRST AID KIT

- ☐ First aid pocket guide
- ☐ 18 cleansing wipes
- ☐ Antiseptic
- ☐ Antibiotic cream
- ☐ Adhesive bandages, assortment
- ☐ Tension bandage
- ☐ Safety pins
- ☐ Roll of gauze
- ☐ Gauze pads
- ☐ Adhesive tape
- ☐ Butterfly closures
- ☐ Cotton tip applicators
- ☐ Tongue depressors
- ☐ 2 pairs vinyl gloves
- ☐ 1 face shield
- ☐ Pair of scissors
- ☐ Ice pack
- ☐ Pencil, notepad
- ☐ Antihistamines
- ☐ Hot water bottle
- ☐ Child Emergency Information Cards (pg. 86)

The Canadian Pharmacists Association suggests that every spring you clean out your medicine cabinet. Remove the following:

- Prescription medicines that are old or that you no longer take
- Old or expired nonprescription medicine
- Medicines no longer in their original containers or with labels you can't read
- Medicines that have changed colour, smell or taste
- Take these medecines back to your pharmacy for safe disposal

▼ FIRST AID FOR EMERGENCIES

St. John Ambulance

The following list of emergency first aid treatments for adults and children has been graciously supplied by St. John Ambulance

To handle an emergency situation, use Emergency Scene Management (ESM).

PERFORM A SCENE SURVEY

1. Take charge.
2. Call out for help.
3. Assess hazards and make the area safe.
4. Find out what happened and the mechanism of injury.
5. Identify yourself and offer to help.
6. If head/spinal injuries are suspected, support the head and neck.
7. Assess responsiveness.
8. Send or go for medical help.

Note: Protect yourself and others by wearing vinyl gloves when giving first aid. Use a shield or face mask with a one-way valve when giving AR or CPR.

BLEEDING

To control severe bleeding:

1. Apply direct pressure to the wound over a pad of dressings if available.
2. Lay the child down and elevate the limb.
3. If the pad of dressings becomes bloodsoaked, do not remove it. Put another one on top and continue pressure until bleeding is controlled.
4. Bandage dressings in place to continue pressure.

MINOR CUTS AND SCRAPES:

1. Wash area with soap and water.
2. Bandage only if necessary. Air promotes healing.

ONGOING CASUALTY CARE

Keep the casualty in the best possible condition until medical help takes over. Give prompt first aid for SHOCK.

1. Reassure the child and handle gently.
2. Loosen tight clothing.
3. Give nothing by mouth.
4. If injuries permit, place the conscious child on the back with feet raised about 30 cm (12 in.). Turn an unconscious child into the recovery position.
5. Cover to keep warm.
6. Recheck the child's condition often.

BURNS

Burns to infants and young children are always serious.

1. Immediately place the burned part in cool water.
2. Remove any tight items, e.g. rings, footwear, bracelets, etc., from the burned area before swelling begins.
3. When the pain is reduced, cover the burn with clean, preferably sterile dressings and bandage lightly.
4. Monitor breathing when burns are around the face.
5. Get medical help.

Do not

- apply butter, ointments or lotions.
- break blisters.
- breathe, cough over or touch the burned area.

POISONING

1. Try to find out:
   - What was swallowed?
   - How much was taken?
   - When it was taken?
2. Immediately call your local Poison Information Centre or emergency number and follow the directions given.

If medical help cannot be reached...

3. Wipe any poisonous material from the face and mouth. If the casualty is conscious, rinse out the mouth. If the casualty is or becomes unconscious, turn into the recovery position.
4. Do not induce vomiting or give anything to drink or eat unless directed to do so.

NOSEBLEEDS

1. Seat the child. Have the child lean forward and pinch the soft part of the nose for 10 minutes.
2. Tell the child not to blow the nose for some hours after bleeding has stopped.
3. Get medical help if bleeding continues or starts again.

▼ INFANTS AND CHILDREN

ARTIFICIAL RESPIRATION (AR)

1. Perform a Scene Survey.
2. Place an unresponsive infant or child face up. Open the airway — push back on the forehead and lift the chin.
3. Look, listen and feel for breathing. Check for 3–5 seconds. If not breathing...
4. Make a tight seal over mouth and nose of an infant (under 1 year). Pinch the nostrils of a child (from 1 to 8) and make a tight seal over the mouth. Give 2 slow breaths, just enough to make the chest rise. If chest does not rise, reposition head, check the seals and try again. If the chest still does not rise — see CHOKING.

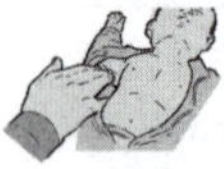

5. If the chest rises, check for a pulse for 5 to 10 seconds — in the arm for an infant, in the neck for a child.
6. If there is a pulse, continue AR, 1 breath every 3 seconds for about 1 minute.

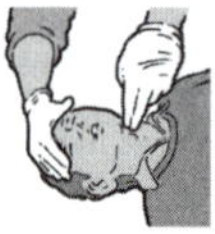

7. If there is no pulse, and you are trained start CPR, otherwise continue AR.
8. Recheck for breathing and for a pulse after one minute and every few minutes after that.

UNCONSCIOUSNESS

Loss of consciousness may threaten life if a child is on his/her back, as the tongue may block the airway.

1. Make sure the child is breathing, then roll into the recovery position.
2. Check breathing often, while waiting for medical help.
3. Never give anything by mouth to an unconscious child.

FOR ADULTS

ARTIFICIAL RESPIRATION (AR – ADULT)

1. Open the airway — push back on the forehead and lift the chin.
2. Look, listen and feel for breathing. Check for 3 to 5 seconds. If the casualty is not breathing...
3. Keep the airway open. Pinch the nostrils and make a tight seal over the mouth. Give 2 slow breaths, enough to make the chest rise. If the chest does not rise, reposition the head, check the seals and try again. If the chest still does not rise... see CHOKING. If the chest does rise...
4. Check for a pulse at the side of the neck for 5 to 10 seconds. If no pulse is felt, and you are trained, start CPR. If a pulse is felt...
5. Continue AR, giving one breath every 5 seconds.

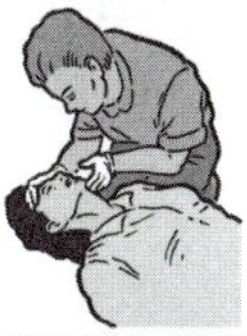

OPEN THE AIRWAY

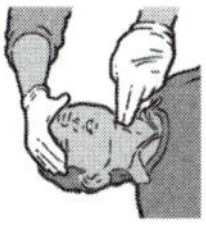

CHECKING FOR A PULSE

BREATHE INTO CASUALTY

Recheck pulse and breathing after one minute and every few minutes after that. Continue AR until the casualty starts breathing or medical help takes over.

UNCONSCIOUSNESS

Loss of consciousness may threaten life if a person is on his back and the tongue has dropped to the back of the throat, blocking the airway. Get medical help. Assess airway, breathing and circulation, place the casualty in the recovery position (see illustration). Never give anything by mouth to an unconscious casualty. Reassess airway, breathing and circulation frequently.

RECOVERY POSITION

CHOKING (ADULT)

If a choking person can speak, breathe or cough — STAND BY and encourage coughing.

If a conscious person cannot speak, breathe or cough:

1. Stand behind the person and find the top of the hip bones with your hands.
2. Place a fist midline against the abdomen.
3. Grasp the fist with the other hand and press inward and upward forcefully.
4. Continue until the object is expelled or the person becomes unconscious.

5. Ease the unconscious person to the ground and send for medical help. If you are alone and a phone is nearby, turn the casualty into the recovery position, get medical help and return. Turn the casualty onto her back.
6. Open the mouth, grasp the jaw with your fingers and lift up. Finger-sweep the mouth with a hooked finger.
7. Tilt the head backward and try to breathe into the casualty. If the chest rises continue AR. If the chest does not rise after the first breath...
8. Reposition the head, check the seals at mouth and nose, and try to breathe into the lungs again. If the chest still does not rise...
9. Kneel across the casualty's legs. Find the top of the hip bones with your hands.
10. Place the heel of one hand midline on the abdomen. Place the other hand on top — fingers raised.
11. Thrust inward and upward up to 5 times. Make each thrust forceful and distinct.
12. Repeat steps 6 to 11 until the object is expelled, the casualty starts breathing or medical help takes over.

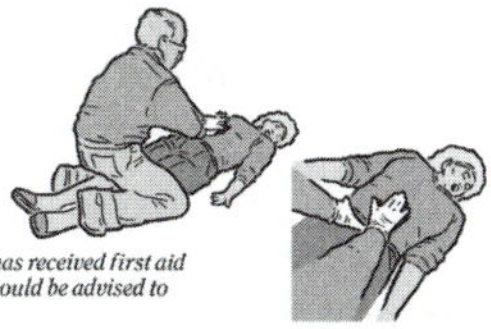

Anyone who has received first aid for choking should be advised to see a doctor.

▼ INFANTS

CHOKING INFANT (UNDER 1 YEAR)

When you see an infant choke on an object or observe:

- serious breathing difficulty
- high-pitched noises
- bluish skin colour.

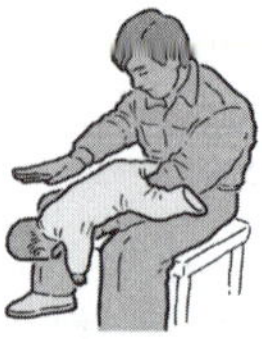

1. Give 5 forceful back blows between the shoulder blades.

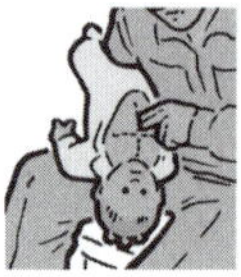

2. Turn the infant onto the back and give 5 chest thrusts using 2 fingertips on the infants breastbone, one finger width below the nippleline. Repeat back blows and chest thrusts until the airway is cleared or the infant becomes unconscious.

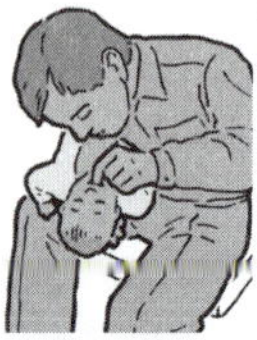

3. If the infant becomes unconscious, send for medical help. Open the mouth, place a finger on the tongue, grasp the chin and lift. Look for and remove only objects you are able to see.

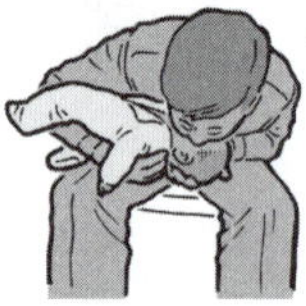

4. Attempt AR. If the chest does not rise, reposition the head and try again. If the chest still does not rise, continue with back blows, chest thrusts, mouth checks, and AR attempts until the chest rises. If the chest rises but the infant does not start to breathe, continue AR.

▼ CHILDREN

CHOKING CHILD (FROM 1 TO 8)

1. If a child can speak, breathe or cough, encourage the child to cough up the object.
2. If a child cannot speak, breathe or cough, stand behind the child and find the top of the hip bones with your hands.
3. Place a fist midline on the abdomen just above the other hand.

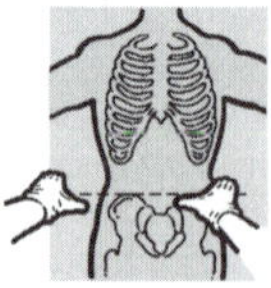

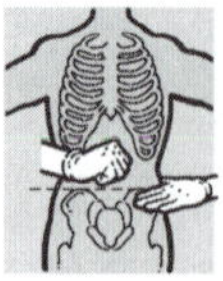

4. Grasp the fist and press inward and upward forcefully. Continue until the object is forced out or the child becomes unconscious.
5. If the child becomes unconscious, lower to the ground. Send for medical help. Open the mouth, and lift the jaw upwards. Look for and remove only objects you can see.

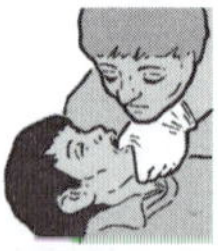

6. If breathing does not start begin AR. If the chest does not rise, reposition the head, check the seals and try again. If the chest still does not rise...
7. Kneel across the child's legs. Place the heel of one hand midline on the abdomen just above the level of the hips. Place the other hand on top and press inward and upward forcefully. Give up to 5 abdominal thrusts.
8. If breathing does not start, continue with mouth checks, AR attempts and abdominal thrusts until the chest rises. If the child does not start to breathe, continue AR.

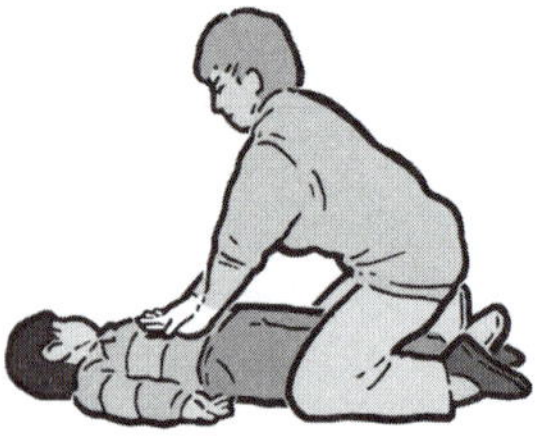

NOTE: This is a step-by-step guide to what you can do until you can get help or medical help arrives. These tips do not take the place of first aid training.

PLAYING IT SAFE

Playing safe ensures the prevention of injuries, which are the No. 1 cause of death and disability in children.

THINGS TO WATCH FOR:

CYCLING

- [ ] Teach the rules of the road.
- [ ] Make sure the bike fits the child.
- [ ] The bike helmet should fit properly and be CSA-approved.

DRIVING

- [ ] Child seats must be properly installed and fit the child. Visit your fire department for help in installing the seat.

IN THE SUN

- [ ] Minimize sun exposure. Schedule outdoor activities when UV rays are weakest — before 11 a.m. and after 4 p.m.
- [ ] Keep children under one out of the sun.
- [ ] Seek natural shade.
- [ ] Cover up with a broad brimmed hat. Protect arms and legs with clothing.
- [ ] Wear a T-shirt over a bathing suit.
- [ ] Use sunscreen that protects against UVA and UVB rays with a sun protection factor (SPF) of at least 15.

WHEN PLAYING

- [ ] Make sure toys are age-appropriate.
- [ ] Remove cords and drawstrings from clothing.
- [ ] In the playground, supervise children under 5 directly; stay close to 5-9 year-olds. Make sure children use the equipment the right way.
- [ ] Always supervise children in, on and around water (in the tub, pool or lake).
- [ ] All children should be taught to swim by a certified swimming instructor.
- [ ] See our section on Sports & Recreation.

Did you know playgrounds installed for use by children aged 18 months to 12 years are ruled by standards? Trouble spots should be reported. Call your playground operator (city parks and recreation department or local school) to let them know about trouble spots. Things to watch for include:

- gaps in play spaces that could cause neck injury
- missing guardrails and barriers to prevent falls
- no protective surfaces to absorb impact and crush falls.

CAUTION! Parents are the best role models. Wear your seatbelt. When biking wear a helmet and follow the rules of the road. Kids will follow your lead.

Children derive many benefits from participating in organized sport or other physical activities. Being active, setting goals, developing physical and mental skills, learning to work within a group, and facing challenges all lead to enhanced self-esteem and personal growth. In recent years, girls have been moving, in increasing numbers, into team sports. These girls will be better prepared to meet the demands of their professional and personal lives, because of the confidence they have gained through their sporting experience.

▾ CHOOSING A SPORT OR ACTIVITY

Sometimes it's relatively simple to decide which sport or activity to enrol your child in. They may express interest in joining a sport or activity or may exhibit a passion for a specific pastime, such as swimming or dance. If their choice is affordable, and an easy commute to a good program, then the decision is clear. For others it's not so obvious. Begin by observing your child at play, making note of when he/she is happiest. If, for instance, your child enjoys learning and being outdoors, but cares little for formal structure and large groups then consider individual non-competitive activities which require the mastery of complex techniques such as golf, skiing, etc. If, on the other hand, your child is happiest working in a group and striving to win, then he is a good candidate for competitive team sports.

Once your child has expressed an interest in a given activity:

▾ CONSIDER THE FOLLOWING

- Current and future financial implications including registration, instruction, equipment, clothing, travel, tournaments, recitals, performances, etc.
- The risks associated with various activities. Be prepared to deal with the downside of your particular choice, i.e. injury rates for sports like hockey and football, or subjective competitive evaluations for sports such as gymnastics or figure skating.
- Remember that some activities are more effective at promoting fitness than are others, i.e. cross-country running vs. bowling.

NOTES

CAUTION! For very young children, guard against moving too fast, either in terms of physical or emotional demands. Even for older children, remain watchful, to ensure that your children's lives remain balanced. There are few things more sad to see than a child who has become disenchanted with a game they once loved, because they have been pushed too hard, too soon, for too long.

- Resist the temptation to push your children into your favorite sport, or the activities that you participated in as a child.

- Resist the urge to 'create' the next junior sports phenom. Sport is worthwhile primarily for the joy it brings the participant, and the character it builds — not for the remote promise of celebrity or wealth 10 or 15 years down the road.

- Finally, encourage your child to participate in both team and individual sports at recreational and competitive levels to round out their experience. For example, a child who is into competitive track and field (individual, competitive) in the summer, could benefit from joining recreational basketball (team, recreational) in the winter.

EVALUATING A TEAM OR PROGRAM

Understanding the difference between recreational and competitive programs can help parents make informed choices. Remember that what separates the two is not the ability of the participants but their disposition. A child with loads of athletic ability who just wants to play and have fun may be best suited to a recreational setting while a child who may not be as gifted but is committed to winning and self-improvement may be more suited to a competitive regime.

RECREATIONAL TEAMS

maximize participation and fun in a friendly atmosphere.

LOOK FOR

- parent coaches (the more the better)
- large team roster
- convenient location training, games
- practices that are fun
- equal time for practices, games

BEWARE OF

- 'win at all cost' coaches
- small team rosters

COMPETITIVE TEAMS

are geared to winning and improving the team's and its members' level of play.

LOOK FOR

- experienced, certified coaches
- parental support in non-coaching positions
- clear understanding of roles within the team
- opportunities for advancement within the team
- more practice time than game time
- most team members of similar abilities
- participation at highest level at which they can be competitive.

BEWARE OF

- teams coached by groups of parents
- teams that focus only on 'key' players
- excessive playing schedule, i.e. too many tournaments

Other parents and former players can be a great source of information for evaluating the programs and coaches that you may be considering, but check a number of sources and remember evaluations of this sort are subjective. Finally, are the coaches themselves approachable? They should be willing to give a clear idea of what is expected of your child, and what opportunities there are now and in the future with this team.

▾ UNDERSTANDING YOUR CHILD'S COMMITMENT

ACCEPTING RESPONSIBILITY

Young children can learn to take responsibility for themselves through participation in organized sport and activities.

Let them schedule their games and practices on the More Time Moms family organizer right from the start. Keep a file either in your file system or in your child's room for sporting contacts, schedules, maps, etc. As information from the activity or team comes into the house put it into the file for reference. Once your child is able to maintain the file on his/her own, let him/her do so.

PREPARATION SAVES TIME

Arriving prepared and on time for games and practices is an absolute must but requires a little planning. Let your child take responsibility for his/her equipment. Have your child prepare an equipment checklist on an index card to refer to when packing the sports bag the day before the game, practice, etc. Here is a sample soccer bag list.

- ☐ Cleats
- ☐ Jersey
- ☐ Oranges
- ☐ Extra spikes
- ☐ Shorts
- ☐ Sunscreen
- ☐ Extra laces
- ☐ Warm-up suit
- ☐ Bug spray
- ☐ Shin guards
- ☐ Water bottle
- ☐ Bandages
- ☐ Socks
- ☐ Towel
- ☐ Sandals

Don't wait until the next day. Have your children check their equipment after each use for articles to be laundered, polished, replaced or repaired.

LEARNING TAKES TIME

To understand a game and appreciate an individual's place within a team takes time. Many sports involve the execution of complex and challenging skills which can only be learned through progressive steps.

However, patience is rarely a characteristic of the young. Parents can play an important role in keeping their children motivated by letting them know that they can see progress even when (or especially when) the child may not. Of course, to do this a parent has to actually observe games or practices.

If a child is becoming discouraged, take him/her to watch a slightly older team or athlete and remind the child that those hotshots out there were, not so long ago, right where he/she is now.

▼ PARENTAL SUPPORT

Sports teams and other activity groups depend largely on the support of parent volunteers. Besides acting as instructors and supervisors, parents can be team managers, fundraisers, registration, event, promotion and communications volunteers. Most of these functions require little if any expertise in the sport or activity itself. Unfortunately, parents can get caught up trying to help and end up doing more harm than good. The following may help.

SUPPORTING YOUR CHILD

DO

- Get your children where they have to be, on time.
- Give praise where appropriate, for effort as well as for results.
- Take time to watch your child at games, practices and recitals.
- Schedule time to speak with the coach or instructor about your child's progress, but not right before or after a game or practice.

DON'T

- Criticize your child's performance or compare him/her to their teammates.
- Add other incentives, such as paying for scoring or other accomplishments.
- Withdraw playing privileges as a discipline for shortcomings at school or other areas — cut down on TV time instead or on social activities.

SUPPORTING YOUR CHILD'S TEAM OR GROUP

DO

- Feel free to praise your child's coaches and teammates.
- Offer to help out with rides or carpooling.
- Accept and appreciate your child's position within the team or group.
- Promote the team or group in your community, at your workplace, in local media.
- Foster the idea that the team or group is the master of its own destiny.

DON'T

- Criticize your child's teammates or coaches, on or away from the field.
- Fall in with a particular parental clique (i.e. the substitutes, the first string etc.).
- Promote unreasonable expectations for the group.
- Focus on things out of your child's or team's control (i.e. officials, opposition, etc.)
- Coach or referee from the sidelines.

CAUTION!

One of the biggest mistakes a parent can make is to shield their children from the disappointments and hard lessons that are part and parcel of the sporting experience. If your child is not performing well or working hard enough in training, then the playing time should be reduced. If they make mistakes that hurt the team, allow them to face the consequences. It may be hard for the parent but in the long run the children will be better players and stronger persons.

NEW PARENT TIPS

Congratulations! We've assembled some of our best baby tips to help you with the arrival of your little one and help you cope with the changes in your life that come along with having a baby. Even if you are not having a baby you can use this section to shop for or support someone in your life who is. Before the baby arrives;

MAKE AND FREEZE AS MANY MEALS AS YOU CAN. Stock up on your pantry and pet food supplies.

HIRE A STUDENT TO COME AFTER SCHOOL to take the older children out to play for awhile after the baby arrives. If you choose to do so, have the student come a few times before the baby arrives to get the children used to his/her company.

FIND GROCERY STORES THAT DELIVER. Some stores offer phone-in or Internet grocery order services, with delivery on a weekly basis. Find out which day of the week it is and pencil it in on your calendar for future reference.

BECOME FAMILIAR WITH CONSIGNMENT AND THRIFT STORES in your area. You can really save on good-quality baby clothes. Consignment stores have lots of clothes in smaller sizes that are relatively new or unused, because babies outgrow their clothes so quickly. Return often, this will be a valuable source of baby wear through your children's growing years.

MAKE SURE YOUR BABY EQUIPMENT PASSES GOVERNMENT SAFETY CODES. This includes cribs, car seats, high chairs, strollers, changing tables, playpens, and safety gates. This tip is often forgotten when the item is borrowed from a friend, passed down from an older child or bought second-hand. Baby equipment should be installed according to manufacturer's directions and checked periodically.

DELAY BUYING YOUR BABY CLOTHES until close to your delivery date and after most gifts have been received. Buy the minimum and keep all baby clothes tagged or in their original packages, so that you can unwrap them as you need them and can return or exchange unused items for a larger size or different color, if necessary. Keep the baby's birthing season in mind when making your clothing choices.

Obtain or consider the following:

Birth certificate	Will	RESP, education fund
Social security number	Legal guardian	Savings account
Passport		Life insurance policy

GETTING READY FOR BABY

FIRST WARDROBE

- [ ] 3 to 7 undershirts
- [ ] 3 to 8 nighties
- [ ] 4 to 6 sleepers
- [ ] 2 to 3 booties, socks
- [ ] 2 to 6 all-in-ones
- [ ] 2 washable bibs
- [ ] 1 to 3 sweaters
- [ ] 1 to 3 hats
- [ ] 1 bunting bag, snowsuit, fleece suit
- [ ] Disposable diapers
- [ ] ....
- [ ] ....

LINEN WARDROBE

- [ ] 3-12 receiving blankets
- [ ] 3 or 4 fitted sheets
- [ ] 2 quilted mattress pads
- [ ] 2-6 waterproof pads
- [ ] 1 crib blanket
- [ ] 1 crib comforter
- [ ] 1 blanket for stroller
- [ ] 1 blanket for car seat
- [ ] 3 towels with hoods
- [ ] 16 wash cloths
- [ ] Cloth diapers and liners
- [ ] ....
- [ ] ....
- [ ] ....

BABY TOILETRIES

- [ ] Baby soap
- [ ] Baby shampoo
- [ ] Baby oil
- [ ] Baby cornstarch
- [ ] Diaper rash ointment
- [ ] Petroleum jelly
- [ ] Diaper wipes
- [ ] Sterile cotton balls
- [ ] Cotton tip applicators
- [ ] Baby scissors or nail clippers
- [ ] Baby brush or comb
- [ ] ....
- [ ] ....
- [ ] ....

FEEDING SUPPLIES

BREAST-FED BABY

- [ ] Breast pump, sterilizer
- [ ] 1 bottle with nipple for water
- [ ] 3 bottles(4-oz.) — supplemental
- [ ] ....
- [ ] ....

BOTTLE-FED BABY

- [ ] Utensils for formula preparation
- [ ] 4 to 6 bottles (4-oz.)
- [ ] 10 to 12 bottles (8-oz.)
- [ ] ....
- [ ] ....

BABY'S MEDICINE CABINET

- [ ] Infant acetaminophen
- [ ] Liquefied charcoal
- [ ] Ipecac syrup
- [ ] Antiseptic cream
- [ ] Hydrogen peroxide
- [ ] Saline drops
- [ ] Calamine lotion
- [ ] Herbal Cort
- [ ] Rehydration fluid
- [ ] Rubbing alcohol
- [ ] Sterile bandages
- [ ] Gauze pads
- [ ] Adhesive tape
- [ ] Tweezers
- [ ] Nasal aspirator
- [ ] Cold mist vaporizer
- [ ] Rectal thermometer
- [ ] Heating pad or hotwater bottle

FOR MOM

- [ ] Vitamin E capsules
- [ ] Lanolin
- [ ] Acetaminophen

When planning the nursery or buying newborn baby clothes, stick to neutral colors for your decorating scheme (yellow, green, purple, ivory or white) and add pink or blue accents when you learn the sex of the baby or the next baby comes along. Keep paint chips and swatches in your planner for easy reference.

NURSERY NEEDS

- [ ] Bassinet or cradle
- [ ] Crib, bumper pads
- [ ] Musical mobile
- [ ] Baby Monitor
- [ ] ....
- [ ] Cool mist humidifier or vaporizer
- [ ] Diaper pail
- [ ] Rocking chair
- [ ] Dresser
- [ ] ....
- [ ] Changing table or tabletop
- [ ] Lamp
- [ ] Hamper
- [ ] ....

ROOM MEASUREMENTS	WINDOW MEASUREMENTS

COLORS	THEME

TRIP TO THE HOSPITAL

FOR THE LABOUR

- [ ] Cash for cab fare, parking
- [ ] Watch or clock with second hand for timing contractions
- [ ] Notebook, pen
- [ ] Insurance form, card
- [ ] Medicare card
- [ ] Hospital admittance form
- [ ] Change for telephone, snacks
- [ ] Small paper bag — hyperventilation
- [ ] Massage lotion, lip balm
- [ ] Tennis ball, rolling pin — massage
- [ ] Sugarless lollipops
- [ ] Music
- [ ] Heavy socks
- [ ] Colored washcloth
- [ ] Sandwiches, snacks for dad
- [ ] Camera, film
- [ ] Video camera, film

AFTER DELIVERY

- [ ] Address book, list of friends to call
- [ ] Calling card
- [ ] Robe
- [ ] 2 or 3 nightgowns, T-shirts
- [ ] Slippers
- [ ] Soap, deodorant, shampoo
- [ ] Toothbrush, toothpaste
- [ ] Cosmetics, perfume
- [ ] Blow dryer, hair accessories
- [ ] Glasses or contact lenses
- [ ] Sanitary napkins
- [ ] Playing cards, books, magazines
- [ ] Snacks
- [ ] Champagne and glasses
- [ ] ....
- [ ] ....
- [ ] ....

COMING HOME

FOR MOM

- [ ] Nursing bra
- [ ] Underwear
- [ ] Shoes
- [ ] Going home outfit
- [ ] Coat or sweater

FOR SIBLING

- [ ] Gift from new baby

FOR BABY

- [ ] Disposable diapers (hospital may supply)
- [ ] Undershirt
- [ ] Sleeper or nightie
- [ ] Socks or booties
- [ ] Receiving blanket
- [ ] Warm blanket
- [ ] Sweater and cap
- [ ] Bunting, snowsuit or fleece suit
- [ ] Infant car seat

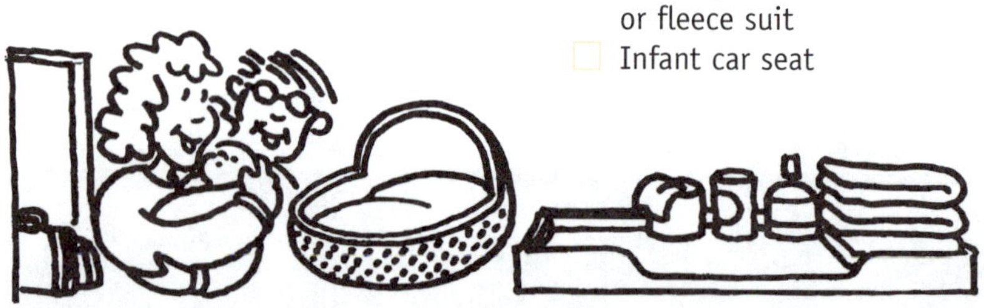

BABY ON THE GO

DIAPER BAG

- [ ] Diapers
- [ ] Baby wipes
- [ ] Diaper cream
- [ ] Tissues
- [ ] Receiving blanket
- [ ] Baby blanket
- [ ] Pacifier
- [ ] Infant acetaminophen
- [ ] Extra outfit
- [ ] Bottles and formula or bottle and water
- [ ] Wet facecloth in plastic bag
- [ ] Rattle or toy
- [ ] Baby bonnet or sun hat
- [ ] Snack for Mom
- [ ] Small plastic bags for soiled clothes or dirty diapers
- [ ] ....
- [ ] ....

FOR OLDER BABIES

- [ ] Teething ring
- [ ] Teething biscuits
- [ ] Snack and juice
- [ ] Bib
- [ ] Sunscreen

OVERNIGHT ESSENTIALS

- [ ] Travelling crib or play yard
- [ ] Crib sheets and blankets
- [ ] Night light
- [ ] Baby monitor
- [ ] Baby carrier or backpack
- [ ] Umbrella stroller
- [ ] Books
- [ ] Favorite sleeping toy
- [ ] First aid kit
- [ ] ....
- [ ] ....
- [ ] ....
- [ ] ....

ON THE ROAD OR IN THE AIR

For long trips, babies and young children can get restless, so pack a few surprises to keep them entertained and pull them out as you need them.

- [ ] New books
- [ ] I Spy books
- [ ] Activity, coloring, sticker books
- [ ] Doodle pads
- [ ] Flash cards
- [ ] Erasable pads
- [ ] Song, story tapes
- [ ] ....
- [ ] ....

FILL OUT THE INFORMATION CARD ON PAGE 54 AND KEEP IT IN YOUR DIAPER BAG. UPDATE IT EVERY THREE MONTHS FOR BABIES UP TO A YEAR AND EVERY SIX MONTHS AFTER THAT

BABY INFORMATION CARD	
NAME	
BIRTHDATE	
WEIGHT	
MEDICAL CARD NO.	
IMMUNIZATION RECORD	
DATE OF LAST TETANUS	
MEDICATIONS	
ALLERGIES	

▼ LEAVING BABY

Fill out the caregiver information form in your Little Helper.
Post it at your message center and show your caregiver where it is.
Review the following things with your sitter before you leave.

▼ SHOW YOUR SITTER

- [ ] Baby's schedule
- [ ] How to give bottle
- [ ] How baby is burped
- [ ] What baby can eat or drink
- [ ] How baby is most calmed
- [ ] How you put baby to sleep
- [ ] How baby sleeps
- [ ] Baby's favorite toy
- [ ] How to diaper baby
- [ ] Where diaper supplies are kept
- [ ] Where baby's clothes are kept
- [ ] Baby's special needs
- [ ] Rules concerning baby and pets
- [ ] Baby safety rules
- [ ] Your visitor policy
- [ ] Pertinent info about the house, setup, alarm, business, phone, etc.
- [ ] Emergency information sheet
- [ ] What to do in case of fire
- [ ] ....

▼ SHOW YOUR SITTER WHERE TO FIND:

- [ ] First aid kit
- [ ] Flashlights and candles
- [ ] Emergency cab fare, taxi phone no.
- [ ] ....
- [ ] Address of the nearest emergency room and the best way to get there
- [ ] Phone number where you will be
- [ ] ....

WHEN BABY ARRIVES

◆ Get help from family and friends or consider hiring someone to assist you with the other children, meal preparation, pets and household tasks. ◆ Record an outgoing message on the answering machine with vital baby info, to save you from answering the phone or returning calls right away. ◆ Cook in double batches when you do cook. ◆ Rest and sleep as often as you can. ◆ Babies rest more easily when they can smell their mother's scent. Leave one of your unlaundered shirts with your caregiver or in baby's crib so he'll sleep longer. ◆ Running water or playing prerecorded sounds of water calm, fussy babies. Taking care of a new baby is demanding and introducing the baby into the family can put additional stress on relationships. Invest some time in yourself and in your other family members. Here are a few suggestions:

MOM AND DAD	MOM	BROTHERS, SISTERS
Dine together	Take a bath	Spend time together
Make time for each other	Read a book	Get someone to take them out
Help each other	Eat well	Let them help with baby
Thank each other	Get regular exercise	Thank them for their help

MORE TIME MOMS BEST BABY AIDS

◆ Infant car seat: preferred models easily detach from the base and act as a baby carrier, a must for sleeping babies. *(0 to 6 months)*. ◆ Sling: by far the most useful piece of baby equipment, it allows you to carry baby comfortably and is convenient to breast-feeding. *(newborn to 1 year)*. ◆ Folding stroller: get the best quality you can afford and make sure the stroller folds down so baby can lie down. *(Newborn to 3 years)*. ◆ Musical mobile: part of baby's sleeping ritual, it plays music and provides motion for baby stimulation. *(0-9 months)*. ◆ Vibrating bouncy seat: new parents swear by this versatile calming chair. *(Newborn to 9 months)*. ◆ Swing: Calms baby but keeps you in view and within earshot, and allows you to do other tasks. *(3-6 months)*. Borrow this item if you can; you will only use it for a short while. ◆ Exer-saucer: baby loves this mobile play station for independence and entertainment. *(4-12 months)*. ◆ Baby carrier or backpack: babies tend to cry less if they are carried around a lot. ◆ Mini food processor: Makes quick work of preparing fresh baby meals, with small quantities and easy cleanup. ◆ Activity walker: provides baby with activity center for developing small motor skills and helps baby become mobile (gross motor skills) at the pre-walking stage. *(6 months to 1 year)*.

BABY'S CELEBRATION

1. When planning this event, keep in mind baby's feeding schedule and sibling's nap time so that everything runs as smoothly as possible.
2. Try to feed baby just before the ceremony so that baby is calmer during the event.
3. Use a caterer at this event, if you can afford it. If any event is worth the additional cost, it is this one. Once you add up the costs of meal preparation and factor in the hassles and limited time, the cost may seem reasonable.
4. If you decide against a caterer, buy as much prepared food as possible and ask family and close friends to bring something. You will require all your energy for the baby and the event.
5. Delegate tasks to as many people as possible, so that you can concentrate on the baby and enjoy the event. Assign someone to:

- ☐ Take coats ....
- ☐ Lay out the food ....
- ☐ Take pictures ....
- ☐ Record gifts and givers as you open them ....
- ☐ Tend bar ....
- ☐ Entertain children ....
- ☐ Videotape ....
- ☐ Clean up ....

BEFORE BABY'S CELEBRATION

- ☐ Talk to priest or rabbi
- ☐ Choose godparents
- ☐ Guest list
- ☐ ....
- ☐ Invitations, maps
- ☐ Decorations
- ☐ Christening favors
- ☐ ....
- ☐ Menu
- ☐ Caterer
- ☐ Enlist help with food
- ☐ ....

FAMILY OUTFITS

- ☐ Baby ....
- ☐ Christening outfit ....
- ☐ Brothers ....
- ☐ Sisters ....
- ☐ Mom ....
- ☐ Dad ....

....

Date: Time:

Place, ceremony:

Place, reception:

MENU PLANNER	DISH	WHERE'S THE RECIPE?
Appetizers		
Hot dishes		
Cold dishes		
Salads		
Condiments		
Sweet table		
Cake		
Beverages		
Table setting(s)		

▼ DON'T FORGET

- [ ] Video camera
- [ ] Camera
- [ ] Film
- [ ] Thank you notes

GUEST LIST, GIFT REGISTRY AND NOTES

AROUND THE HOUSE & GARAGE

Now that your child can roll over and crawl, making a few alterations to your home will protect him and give you peace of mind, if for some reason, he slips from view. It's one thing to chase around after him at grandma's house catching works of art as you go, but it is another to be on watch 24 hours a day in your own home. The following should cover all your bases.

▼ STORE LOCKED OR OUT OF REACH

- [ ] Poisonous, caustic substances
- [ ] Sharp objects
- [ ] Plastic bags, plastic wrap, foil wrap
- [ ] Choking hazards — small things
- [ ] Small electrical appliances
- [ ] Knick-knacks, breakables
- [ ] Poisonous houseplants
- [ ] Garden tools, automotive supplies
- [ ] Hazardous chemicals and paints

▼ ELECTRICAL, HEATING SYSTEMS

- [ ] Run electrical cords under carpets or nail them along baseboards
- [ ] Cover electrical outlets
- [ ] Grills for heaters, fireplaces, etc.
- [ ] Smoke detectors outside bedrooms — at least one per floor, test regularly
- [ ] Remove space heaters — leading cause of serious burns to children

▼ FURNISHINGS

- [ ] Stabilize, remove unstable furniture
- [ ] Tighten, remove loose knobs
- [ ] Protect sharp edges, corner guards
- [ ] Fasten bookcases to the wall
- [ ] Store TVs, heavy items a child can pull down in cabinets or high shelf

▼ KITCHEN

- [ ] Store food in childproof containers
- [ ] Keep garbage in a securely locked cabinet or tightly sealed container
- [ ] Install appliance latches on ovens and microwaves

▼ WINDOWS AND DOORS

- [ ] Install window guards or locks
- [ ] Move furniture away from windows
- [ ] Tie up or shorten drapery cords
- [ ] Closet doors open from inside
- [ ] Keep outside doors locked
- [ ] Lock access to basement, garage
- [ ] Keep control switch on automatic doors and the remote control out of reach; make sure that your garage door's reverse mechanism works.

▼ BATHROOMS

- [ ] Remove medications from reach
- [ ] Toilet lid latch
- [ ] Hot water thermostat @ 120F or 49C
- [ ] Protective cover on water spout
- [ ] Skid-proof inside of tub
- [ ] Place a non-skid rug next to the tub
- [ ] Make sure you can unlock and open door from outside
- [ ] Install interruptors on electrical outlets
- [ ] Never leave your child unattended in the bathtub
- [ ] Never leave water in the tub when not in use; drownings can occur in one inch of water

YOUR HOME

OUTDOORS

- [ ] Never leave an infant or toddler outdoors alone
- [ ] Check for potential hazards - glass, wobbly railings, sharp edges, peeling paint
- [ ] Fence off garbage cans so child can't go exploring
- [ ] Store pails, empty flowerpots and wading pools upside down
- [ ] Remove or fence poisonous plants
- [ ] Check outdoor play equipment for sturdiness, anchoring, sharp edges
- [ ] Keep doors to balcony, deck locked
- [ ] Check wooden deck floors and fences periodically for splinters
- [ ] Railing slats — less than 3.5″ apart
- [ ] Seal gaps 3″ or larger between bottom of fence and ground

STAIRWAYS

- [ ] Safety gates, top and bottom
- [ ] Secure banisters and railings; uprights s/b less than 5" apart
- [ ] Remove area rugs at staircase

NURSERY

- [ ] Keep monitor on when baby is alone
- [ ] Use a crib manufactured after 1989 that meets current safety standards
- [ ] Use a changing table with high sides and a safety strap
- [ ] Keep vaporizers out of reach; cool mist vaporizers are safer
- [ ] Outside lock on door to keep younger siblings out while baby sleeps

SWIMMING POOL

- [ ] Fence in and lock gates to swimming pools
- [ ] Install non-slip material around the pool
- [ ] Install ground-fault circuit interrupters on electrical outlets near the pool
- [ ] Ensure that the pool area is well lit at night
- [ ] Secure pool cover over the pool during the winter months, making sure there are no spaces through which child could slip.

KEEP THESE NEARBY

- [ ] Non-metal reaching pole
- [ ] Throwing line with buoyant aid
- [ ] First-aid kit
- [ ] Telephone, emergency #'s

TO PICK UP

QUANTITY REQUIRED

- [ ] ___ Electrical outlet covers
- [ ] ___ Childproof latches
- [ ] ___ Cushioned corner covers
- [ ] ___ Cord shorteners for blinds and electrical cords
- [ ] ___ Doorknob covers
- [ ] ___ Safety gates; stairs, decks, etc.
- [ ] ___ VCR lock
- [ ] ___ Window guards
- [ ] ___ Toilet latches
- [ ] ___ Cushioned faucet guard
- [ ] ___ Slip-proof appliques or mat
- [ ] ___ Glass fireplace screen
- [ ] ___ ....
- [ ] ___ ....
- [ ] ___ ....

▾ DAYCARE, NANNIES & BABYSITTERS

Finding the ideal child care provider for you and your family can be one challenge that will seem daunting at times. Our step-by-step approach will guide you. We will help you get started, assist with your search and help you get settled in your new child care arrangements.

WHAT IS QUALITY CHILDCARE?

Childcare should support a child's emotional, social, intellectual and physical well-being. Quality childcare is not babysitting.

CAREGIVERS ARE KEY TO QUALITY CHILDCARE. THEY SHOULD...

- understand how children grow and learn
- be affectionate and responsive, open and informative
- provide a stable and stimulating environment
- seek out community resources and support
- be willing to develop common goals

QUALITY CHILDCARE SETTINGS HAVE COMMON CHARACTERISTICS...

- clean, safe and secure
- a caring, learning environment
- space for quiet and active teams, indoor and outdoor play
- a balance of interesting activities
- flexible yet predictable daily routine
- a variety of easily available toys and equipment
- nutritional meals and snacks

Source: The Canadian Child Care Federation

Regulation of childcare varies from state to territory to province. Find out how care is regulated in your area and whether you are eligible for subsidized care by checking the blue pages in the telephone book. Child resource centers or your local community center will have the information you need.

The tax system is different in many jurisdictions. In some cases, child care expenses can lead to a refundable tax credit or other type of deduction. Find out what the ceiling is for your situation from your accountant or local tax center.

▼ STEP 1 — GETTING STARTED

FINDING THE IDEAL CHILDCARE PROVIDER SITUATION

▼ USE THIS CHECKLIST TO IDENTIFY YOUR NEEDS

- [ ] I have a regular work schedule.
- [ ] I sometimes need evening and weekend care.
- [ ] I need care that is close to my work.
- [ ] I travel a lot.
- [ ] My work schedule is unpredictable.
- [ ] Caregivers must be on my bus route to work.
- [ ] My partner can share the driving.
- [ ] I have preschool and school-age children requiring after-school care.
- [ ] My child has special needs (e.g. diet, health, etc.).
- [ ] Language is important to me.
- [ ] Finances are tight.
- [ ] I can share caregivers with a neighbor or friend.
- [ ] I have one child. Playmates are important to me.
- [ ] ....
- [ ] ....

▼ STEP 2 — THE SEARCH

SCREENING

Once you have a list of potential caregivers, it may be a good idea to conduct telephone interviews. Write your questions down and ask the same questions to all caregivers. Check your questions against the needs you identified.

▼ HERE'S A SUGGESTED LIST OF QUESTIONS TO ASK:

- [ ] How many children do you have in your care? What are the ages?
- [ ] How long have you been caring for children?
- [ ] Who are the other members of the household?
- [ ] Are they at home during care hours?
- [ ] What is your daily routine?
- [ ] What are the hours?
- [ ] Do you have first aid certification? CPR?
- [ ] Are there pets in the house? Smokers?
- [ ] What are the costs? Does this include meals, snacks?
- [ ] What kind of meals do you serve?
- [ ] Do you have liability insurance in case of accident?
- [ ] When can I visit?
- [ ] ....
- [ ] ....

INTERVIEWING

- [ ] Can you tell me about yourself? Can you tell me why you chose caregiving?
- [ ] What can you tell about your caregiving style?
- [ ] What training or experience do you have working with children?
- [ ] What kind of things do you like doing with children?
- [ ] Tell me about your daily routine.
- [ ] How do you comfort crying babies, unhappy children?
- [ ] What do you consider unacceptable behaviour?
- [ ] How would you discipline a child?
- [ ] How about outings?
- [ ] Do you travel by bus, by car?
- [ ] How old is your car?
- [ ] Do you have car seats/seatbelts for all the children?
- [ ] Do you take children outdoors every day?
- [ ] In the winter?
- [ ] What kind of games do the children play outside?
- [ ] Is your yard fenced in?
- [ ] Is your pool closed off to children?
- [ ] How much television do the children watch?
- [ ] Can you show me examples of the kinds of crafts the children work on?
- [ ] Do you fit housework into your daily schedule?
- [ ] What is your policy on sick children?
- [ ] What is the cost? How is payment made?
- [ ] How much advance notice do you require for vacation?
- [ ] What is your policy on payment when the children are away?
- [ ] Do you have backup arrangements?
- [ ] Would you consult us if you were considering increasing the number of children in your care?
- [ ] Where do you keep your cleaning supplies? Medications?
- [ ] Would you let me or my partner make unscheduled visits?
- [ ] Can you supply the names and telephone numbers of people whose children you have cared for in the past? Those you are currently caring for?

You will want to follow up the personal interview with a visit to the facilities with your child, if your caregiver is not coming to your home. Specific things to look for are safety hazards including safety gates at the top and bottom of stairs, play and quiet-time spots, the quality of the food served, cleanliness and clutter. If you are bringing someone into your home, you will want him/her to spend some time with your child during the interview so you can observe his/her manner with your child.

CHECKING REFERENCES

Name of caregiver: ....

Name of reference: ....

Dates provided care: .... to ....

and age of children: ....

Reason care was ended: ....

	POOR	AVERAGE	EXCEEDED EXPECTATIONS
Was caregiver reliable?	☐	☐	☐
Arrived on time?	☐	☐	☐
Left early frequently?	☐	☐	☐
Attitude?	☐	☐	☐
Accepted responsibility?	☐	☐	☐
Was organized?	☐	☐	☐
Interaction with parents?	☐	☐	☐
Kept parents informed?	☐	☐	☐
Followed instructions?	☐	☐	☐
Organized age-appropriate activities?	☐	☐	☐
Served healthy quality meals and snacks?	☐	☐	☐
Had a predictable routine?	☐	☐	☐

What was her fee? ....

Any concerns? ....

Would you hire her again? Why? ....

....

STEP 3 — SETTLING IN

- ☐ Be clear with your expectations; ask the provider about hers.
- ☐ Respect the provider's role. Trust her skill.
- ☐ Be on time.
- ☐ Maintain open two-way communication.
- ☐ Ask for and get regular reports on child activities.
- ☐ Make sure your provider has the information she needs to do her work.
- ☐ Review emergency information and routines before he begins, Little Helper.
- ☐ Remember to put emergency child information cards in your first aid kit, p. 86.
- ☐ Tell her about baby's special needs and habits.
- ☐ Let caregiver know when you should be called at work.
- ☐ Ask for sufficient notice of schedule changes.
- ☐ Give lots of notice if your vacation or work schedule changes.
- ☐ Voice concerns. Express appreciation.
- ☐ Write a contract or letter of agreement — it can save unnecessary misunderstanding. Fulfill your part of the agreement.

GETTING AWAY

DAY TRIPS AND OUTINGS

Plan to spend a lot of time with your family on little outings throughout the year. To keep things fun and stimulating you should plan a different family outing once a week. Tailor day trips to the age and interest of your children. Whether it's a day, an afternoon or just a couple of hours, it's the planning that determines the success or failure of an outing with children. Check your local visitor's centre for tourist attractions and community events.

- Amusement parks
- Aquarium
- Art gallery
- Beach
- Bus excursions
- Circus
- City walks
- Country rambles
- Horseback riding
- Fairs
- Farm
- Ferry rides
- Fishing
- Golf
- Hiking
- Miniature golf
- Movie
- Museums
- Children's museums
- Historical sites
- Planetarium
- Parades
- Parks
- Picnics
- Plays for kids
- Playgrounds
- Puppet shows
- Recreation parks
- Science centres
- Skating
- Skiing
- Snowboarding
- Tobogganing
- Theatre
- Train trips
- Water slides
- Zoo

▼ DAY TRIPS WE ARE GOING TO TAKE THIS YEAR

▼ A DAY AT THE BEACH

- ☐☐☐☐ A well-packed cooler
- ☐☐☐☐ Bathing suits — bright colours for kids
- ☐☐☐☐ Beach chairs
- ☐☐☐☐ Beachwear
- ☐☐☐☐ Beach towels, one per person + 1
- ☐☐☐☐ Beach umbrella, wind screen
- ☐☐☐☐ Cover-up, extra shirts
- ☐☐☐☐ Disposable diapers
- ☐☐☐☐ Life jackets, water-wings
- ☐☐☐☐ Sandals, water shoes
- ☐☐☐☐ Sand toys
- ☐☐☐☐ Sun hats, caps
- ☐☐☐☐ Sunscreen, lip balm, zinc oxide
- ☐☐☐☐ Sweaters or sweatshirts
- ☐☐☐☐ Water bottles, one each
- ☐☐☐☐ Water toys
- ☐☐☐☐ ____________
- ☐☐☐☐ ____________
- ☐☐☐☐ ____________

▼ PICNICS

- ☐☐☐☐ A well-packed cooler
- ☐☐☐☐ Picnic blanket
- ☐☐☐☐ Tablecloth
- ☐☐☐☐ Portable stove
- ☐☐☐☐ Portable radio, cassette, CD
- ☐☐☐☐ Frisbee, ball, volleyball
- ☐☐☐☐ Badminton rackets, net
- ☐☐☐☐ Books, cards
- ☐☐☐☐ Sweaters, sweatshirts
- ☐☐☐☐ Sun hats, caps
- ☐☐☐☐ Sunscreen, lip balm, zinc oxide
- ☐☐☐☐ Insect repellent
- ☐☐☐☐ ____________
- ☐☐☐☐ ____________
- ☐☐☐☐ ____________

▼ A WELL-PACKED COOLER

- ☐☐☐☐ Cups, plates, utensils
- ☐☐☐☐ Corkscrew, bottle opener
- ☐☐☐☐ Multi-purpose knife
- ☐☐☐☐ Water bottles, one each
- ☐☐☐☐ A damp facecloth in a resealable plastic bag
- ☐☐☐☐ Lots of fruit, fruit salad
- ☐☐☐☐ Veggies and dip, salads
- ☐☐☐☐ Sandwiches or picnic chicken
- ☐☐☐☐ Lots to drink
- ☐☐☐☐ ____________
- ☐☐☐☐ ____________

GRANDMA'S PICNIC CHICKEN

- Skin, rinse and pat dry 12 thighs and 12 drumsticks; set aside.
- Place 1/2 cup butter on each of 2 cookie sheets and melt in 375 oven. Don't let the butter burn.
- In a medium sized baggie, combine 1 1/2 cups dry breadcrumbs, 2 tsp. salt, 1 tsp. each of thyme, marjoram, rosemary, pepper and 2 tsp. paprika; set aside.
- Beat 3 eggs and 3 Tbs. cold water in a flat dish; set aside.
- Roll each piece of chicken in the eggs, then shake them in crumbs to coat.
- Place chicken on cookie sheet, turning once to coat with melted butter.
- Cook 30 minutes, turn chicken pieces, cook another 30 minutes. (Freeze, thaw in cooler)

▼ HIKING

▼ ADULT'S BACKPACK

- ☐☐☐☐ Backpack
- ☐☐☐☐ Binoculars
- ☐☐☐☐ Canteen
- ☐☐☐☐ Wineskin, collapsible jug
- ☐☐☐☐ Swiss army knife
- ☐☐☐☐ Nylon rope
- ☐☐☐☐ Pliers
- ☐☐☐☐ Flashlight
- ☐☐☐☐ Map, compass
- ☐☐☐☐ Extra socks; cotton or wool
- ☐☐☐☐ Insect repellent
- ☐☐☐☐ Sunscreen
- ☐☐☐☐ Rainwear
- ☐☐☐☐ Bandana
- ☐☐☐☐ Food and snacks
- ☐☐☐☐ Water bottle
- ☐☐☐☐ Chlorine tablets
- ☐☐☐☐ Matches
- ☐☐☐☐ Whistle — in case you get lost
- ☐☐☐☐ Mini first aid kit, p. 89
- ☐☐☐☐ ____________
- ☐☐☐☐ ____________
- ☐☐☐☐ ____________
- ☐☐☐☐ ____________

▼ CHILD'S BACKPACK

- ☐☐☐☐ Backpack
- ☐☐☐☐ Water bottle
- ☐☐☐☐ Food and snacks
- ☐☐☐☐ Extra socks, cotton or wool
- ☐☐☐☐ Bright polar fleece shell
- ☐☐☐☐ Extra running shoes
- ☐☐☐☐ Rainwear
- ☐☐☐☐ Whistle — in case child is lost
- ☐☐☐☐ ____________
- ☐☐☐☐ ____________
- ☐☐☐☐ ____________
- ☐☐☐☐ ____________

HIKING WITH KIDS

Make sure your child knows what to do if he or she gets lost. Explain precisely how to use the supplies in his backpack. Should your child get separated from the group, make sure he knows to stay put, stay calm and hug a tree. It's easier to find them if they don't move around and they won't risk wandering further astray. Have them put on the brightly colored fleece so they are easier to spot. Use the whistle often to alert rescuers. Three toots is the universal signal for help. Finally, tell kids to help you find them by making huge clues, like giant arrows made of rocks, branches and leaves.

FISHING

- Tackle box
- Fishing rod, poles with string
- Fishing line
- Sinkers
- Bobbers
- Leaders
- Hooks
- Bait
- Knife
- Nail clipper
- Screwdriver
- Life jacket
- Hat, cap
- Sunscreen, lip balm, zinc
- Insect repellent
- Food and beverages
- Rubber boots
- Rainwear
- A well-packed cooler, p. 67
- Mini first aid kit, see p. 89

WINTER DAY TRIP

- Filled hot thermal jug
- Hats, neck warmers
- Helmets
- Gloves, mittens
- Goggles, sunglasses
- Ski jacket, ski pants
- Thermal socks, underwear
- Turtleneck, sweater
- Skis, poles, boots
- Snowboard, board boots
- Toboggan
- Skates, guards
- Snow boots
- Sunscreen, lip balm, zinc ox.
- Water bottles, one each
- A well-packed cooler, p. 67
- Mini first aid kit, p. 89

OTHER DAY TRIPS

CLOTHING

- Hats
- Shirts
- Jackets — snow, rain
- Pants
- Extra socks
- Footwear
- Bathing suit
- Thermal underwear
- Accessories
- Sunglasses, ski goggles

CHILD'S BACKPACK

- Sunscreen, lip balm, zinc
- Insect repellent
- Water bottles, one each
- Special gear, equipment and toys for the activity
- Protection from the elements: rain or beach umbrellas, rainwear, wind screen
- Pocket knife, corkscrew
- A well-packed cooler, p. 67
- Mini first aid kit, p. 89

The more planning you do for your camping trips, the happier you will be with your experience. If a trip across the country is in order, then planning up to a year in advance is not too soon. If you are planning to camp during a long weekend or during high season, you will need to book your site well in advance, as most of the more popular sites fill up early. Good sources of info on campgrounds, services and nearby activities are the Internet, CAA, AAA, KOA and local tourist bureaus. Ask for pictures of the site before booking.

When deciding on a campsite, choose the one that best suits your comfort level and the types of activities you enjoy. Some campgrounds offer conveniences such as a general store, hot showers, pools, beaches, water and electrical hookups, while others do not. Take the time to list the different activities and hobbies you enjoy. Do you want to hike, bike, swim, visit amusement parks or participate in local events? The local tourist center will have information on special events taking place during your stay.

Use the space to the right to plan your trip. You can use the lists that follow for four camping trips. Use the left-most column of check boxes for your first trip.

BY THE WAY Although this section was designed with tent camping in mind, there are other types of camping to consider. If you are using a camping vehicle, just cross out the things on the lists that do not apply.

RV Camping: RVs are a good choice for a longer, cross-country type of vacation. They are veritable homes on wheels that come equipped with everything, including a TV if you choose. Check the yellow pages for rental outlets. While it is true that RVs are expensive and heavy on gas, you don't need a car and you won't have to set up camp. Not all campgrounds admit RVs.

Trailer & Tent Trailer Camping: Trailer camping provides many of the conveniences of home and you get to use your own car for shopping, touring, etc. Tent trailers require set-up and tear-down at the site. Make sure that your vehicle has the proper towing capacity and mirrors for the trailer of your choice and that the campground can accommodate your trailer. Before leaving the rental outlet make sure you are able to set up and operate all parts of the trailer by yourself.

▼ CAMPGROUND INFO

CAMPSITES

Address	
Telephone	Cost
Special Features	
Address	
Telephone	Cost
Special Features	
Address	
Telephone	Cost
Special Features	
Address	
Telephone	Cost
Special Features	

THINGS TO DO ON OUR CAMPING TRIPS

TENT CAMPING: When you book your campsite, specify the number of tents you want to set up on your site. Some campsites will charge for additional tents and some require that you take additional sites.

Before starting out on your trip, set up your tents in the backyard and hose down to inspect for leaks and damage. Repair the tents and spray with protector, paying special attention to the seams. Set up and spray new tents as well. Keep your tent instructions and a patch kit handy during the trip.

You can never have too many waterproof tarps on a camping trip. Cover tents, eating areas and entertainment areas with tarps to stay dry.

Pack your clothing and equipment in waterproof plastic containers. They'll come in handy in case of rain and can be used as tabletops.

Have each child bring his/her own backpack and doodle bag and toiletries. A separate toiletries bag makes trips to the showers much easier.

▼ PACKING FOR CAMPING

Pack your clothing and equipment in waterproof plastic containers. They'll come in handy in case of rain.

▼ GLOVE COMPARTMENT

- ☐☐☐☐ Reservation vouchers
- ☐☐☐☐ Maps
- ☐☐☐☐ Vehicle registration
- ☐☐☐☐ Vehicle rental papers
- ☐☐☐☐ Insurance papers
- ☐☐☐☐ Drivers' licenses
- ☐☐☐☐ Health cards
- ☐☐☐☐ ID — for everyone
- ☐☐☐☐ Travellers cheques
- ☐☐☐☐ Coins — laundry, shower, tolls
- ☐☐☐☐ ....
- ☐☐☐☐ ....
- ☐☐☐☐ ....

▼ TOOLS

- ☐☐☐☐ Small shovel
- ☐☐☐☐ Small hatchet
- ☐☐☐☐ Multi-purpose knife
- ☐☐☐☐ Old newspapers
- ☐☐☐☐ Firewood
- ☐☐☐☐ Dustpan and brush
- ☐☐☐☐ Lantern
- ☐☐☐☐ Flashlights, extra batteries
- ☐☐☐☐ Travel first aid kit, p. 79
- ☐☐☐☐ ....
- ☐☐☐☐ ....
- ☐☐☐☐ ....
- ☐☐☐☐ ....

EMERGENCY CAMPING KIT

Choose a brightly-coloured small toolbox or fishing kit for these items. Just put a little bit of everything in the kit and restock at the end of the trip.

- [ ] Rubber bands
- [ ] Twist ties
- [ ] String
- [ ] Clothespins
- [ ] Plastic bags
- [ ] Tissues
- [ ] Mirror
- [ ] Adhesive bandages
- [ ] Tweezers, nail file
- [ ] Nail clippers
- [ ] Thermometer
- [ ] Cotton swabs, cotton balls
- [ ] Acetaminophen
- [ ] Scotch tape, glue
- [ ] Pen, paper
- [ ] Scissors
- [ ] Empty pill container
- [ ] Compass
- [ ] Nails, screws, tacks
- [ ] Electrical tape
- [ ] Masking tape
- [ ] Retractable knife blade
- [ ] Mini sewing kit
- [ ] Safety pins
- [ ] Buttons
- [ ] Candles
- [ ] Waterproof matches
- [ ] Packets — sugar, salt, pepper
- [ ] Spoon, knife, fork
- [ ] Toothpicks
- [ ] Dice
- [ ] $5.00 in change

BEDDING

- [ ] Sleeping bags
- [ ] Mattresses — air, foam
- [ ] Air pump
- [ ] Cots
- [ ] Blankets, pillows
- [ ] Towels — pack in plastic bin
- [ ] Portable bed — baby, toddler

TENT

- [ ] Tents, instructions
- [ ] Pegs, poles
- [ ] Tarps
- [ ] Groundsheets
- [ ] Rope - heavy duty
- [ ] Tent repair kit

ENTERTAINMENT

- [ ] Deck of cards
- [ ] Puzzle, board game
- [ ] Beach toys, water wings
- [ ] Life jacket
- [ ] Fishing equipment
- [ ] Sporting items
- [ ] Books, magazines
- [ ] Radio, extra batteries
- [ ] Nature books
- [ ] Guitar
- [ ] Football, soccer ball
- [ ] Baseball, bat, gloves

▼ CLOTHING

A doodle bag is a special bag for personal items. An old pillowcase with a placket and string will do the job. One per person makes shower time a breeze.

▼ DOODLE BAG

- [ ] Soap, soap container
- [ ] Toothbrush, paste, floss
- [ ] Deodorant
- [ ] Shampoo
- [ ] Brush, comb, hair ties
- [ ] Shaving kit
- [ ] Shower shoes, flip-flops

▼ KID'S BACKPACK

- [ ] Bathing suit
- [ ] T-shirt, cover-up
- [ ] Cap, wide brimmed hat
- [ ] Extra change of clothes
- [ ] Extra pair of shoes
- [ ] Doodle bag

PACK A SET OF THE FOLLOWING ITEMS FOR EACH FAMILY MEMBER

- [ ] Pants
- [ ] Shorts
- [ ] T-shirts
- [ ] Long sleeve shirts
- [ ] Socks
- [ ] Underwear
- [ ] Thermal underwear
- [ ] Pyjamas
- [ ] Hooded sweatshirt
- [ ] Track or sweatpants
- [ ] Rainwear
- [ ] Sneakers
- [ ] Hiking shoes
- [ ] Sandals
- [ ] One special outfit

DON'T FORGET YOUR OWN BEACH BAG

- [ ] Bathing suits
- [ ] T-shirts, cover-ups
- [ ] Cap, wide-brimmed hat
- [ ] Sunglasses
- [ ] Books
- [ ] Sunscreen
- [ ] Insect repellent

AND

▼ CAMP COOKING

Try not to spend all your time cooking. Use the camping menu to lay out a week of favourite easy meals. You can keep it and reuse it for all your trips.

▼ COOKING EQUIPMENT

- ☐☐☐☐ All-in-one "mess kit" or plastic, paper dishes
- ☐☐☐☐ Forks, spoons, knives
- ☐☐☐☐ Tablecloth, napkins
- ☐☐☐☐ Dishcloths, towels
- ☐☐☐☐ Plastic dishpan
- ☐☐☐☐ Plastic mixing bowls
- ☐☐☐☐ Wooden spoon
- ☐☐☐☐ Small cutting board
- ☐☐☐☐ Paring knife
- ☐☐☐☐ Coolers
- ☐☐☐☐ ....
- ☐☐☐☐ Coffee pot
- ☐☐☐☐ Frying pan, spatula
- ☐☐☐☐ Saucepans — 2 or more
- ☐☐☐☐ Coleman stove, naphtha
- ☐☐☐☐ Barbeque, propane
- ☐☐☐☐ Barbeque utensils, mitts
- ☐☐☐☐ Aluminum foil
- ☐☐☐☐ Small resealable bags
- ☐☐☐☐ Drinking water — 5 gal.
- ☐☐☐☐ ....
- ☐☐☐☐ ....
- ☐☐☐☐ ....

▼ STAPLES

- ☐☐☐☐ Salt, pepper
- ☐☐☐☐ Ketchup, mustard, relish
- ☐☐☐☐ Barbeque sauce, mayo
- ☐☐☐☐ Coffee, tea bags
- ☐☐☐☐ Sugar
- ☐☐☐☐ Butter, peanut butter
- ☐☐☐☐ Herbs and spices
- ☐☐☐☐ ....
- ☐☐☐☐ Dishsoap
- ☐☐☐☐ Laundry soap
- ☐☐☐☐ Veggie peeler
- ☐☐☐☐ Can opener
- ☐☐☐☐ Coolers
- ☐☐☐☐ Ice, ice packs
- ☐☐☐☐ ....
- ☐☐☐☐ ....

▼ CAMPING MEAL IDEAS

- ☐☐☐☐ Eggs, bacon, sausages, ham
- ☐☐☐☐ Pancakes
- ☐☐☐☐ French toast
- ☐☐☐☐ Toast, spreads
- ☐☐☐☐ Bagels and cream cheese
- ☐☐☐☐ Hot dogs
- ☐☐☐☐ Hamburgers
- ☐☐☐☐ Franks and beans
- ☐☐☐☐ Canned soup and sandwiches
- ☐☐☐☐ ....
- ☐☐☐☐ ....
- ☐☐☐☐ ....
- ☐☐☐☐ Chili
- ☐☐☐☐ Spaghetti, pasta dishes
- ☐☐☐☐ Barbeque chicken
- ☐☐☐☐ Shish kebabs
- ☐☐☐☐ Pita bread pizzas
- ☐☐☐☐ Marshmallows
- ☐☐☐☐ S'mores
- ☐☐☐☐ ....
- ☐☐☐☐ ....
- ☐☐☐☐ ....
- ☐☐☐☐ ....
- ☐☐☐☐ ....

If you are bringing the pets along, check first with your campground to see if pets are welcome and then refer to the vacations checklist for things to bring.

Remember to prepare individual "doodle bags" to make washroom and shower time a breeze.

SET UP CAMP AS SOON AS YOU ARRIVE.

- Delegate jobs to get set up quickly; gather wood, set up tents, blow up air mattresses, get event information, etc.
- Pick a high, flat spot on your site to set up your sleeping tents. If you can set up under a tree, do so.
- Set up tarps and flys and dig drainage ditches around the perimeter of your tents for rain runoff. Do this right away, don't wait for the rain.
- Leave your food in the car at night to protect it from foraging animals. Make sure to lock your car doors in the evening to protect your valuables.
- Keep your emergency first aid kit in a handy place, known to everyone.
- Keep the window of the tents open to avoid condensation.
- After setting up camp, check out the local information centre, grocery store and special events calendar to get the lay of the land and make the most of your camping trip.

NOTES

PREPARE A WEEK OF GROCERY LISTS AND MENUS FOR YOUR TRIP.
TEAR IT OUT AND TAKE IT WITH YOU WHEN YOU GO SHOPPING.
ONCE YOU ARE DONE WITH IT, PUT IT BACK IN YOUR PLANNER FOR NEXT TIME.

S
SATURDAY
Breakfast
Lunch
Dinner

S
SUNDAY
Breakfast
Lunch
Dinner

M
MONDAY
Breakfast
Lunch
Dinner

T
TUESDAY
Breakfast
Lunch
Dinner

W
WEDNESDAY
Breakfast
Lunch
Dinner

T
THURSDAY
Breakfast
Lunch
Dinner

F
FRIDAY
Breakfast
Lunch
Dinner

▼ SHOPPING LIST FOR OUR TRIP

SUPPLIES

GROCERIES

ABOUT THE CAR

GETTING READY FOR THE TRIP

It's a good idea to check the car before you leave on your vacation. Doing so can save you time, money on the road.

▼ CHECK TIRES

- ☐☐☐☐ Tread wear
- ☐☐☐☐ Tire pressure; correct tire pressure is marked on your tire

▼ CHECK LIGHTS

- ☐☐☐☐ Brake lights
- ☐☐☐☐ Turn signals
- ☐☐☐☐ Four-way flashers
- ☐☐☐☐ Headlights — high, low

▼ CHECK FLUIDS

- ☐☐☐☐ Transmission oil
- ☐☐☐☐ Engine oil
- ☐☐☐☐ Power steering fluid
- ☐☐☐☐ Brake fluid
- ☐☐☐☐ Windshield washer fluid

▼ CHECK BELTS

- ☐☐☐☐ Power steering
- ☐☐☐☐ Air conditioning
- ☐☐☐☐ Alternator belt; keep the belts you change; they can be used for future emergencies

It's a good idea to keep the following in your vehicle at all times:

▼ EMERGENCY KIT

- ☐☐☐☐ Travel first aid kit
- ☐☐☐☐ Flashlight, batteries
- ☐☐☐☐ Snack food
- ☐☐☐☐ Bottled water
- ☐☐☐☐ Flares — flares should be placed 20 ft from car when used, to avoid oncoming traffic

▼ IN WINTER ADD

- ☐☐☐☐ Blankets
- ☐☐☐☐ Candles, matches
- ☐☐☐☐ Shovel

▼ TRAVEL FIRST AID KIT

- ☐☐☐☐ Acetaminophen, adult, child
- ☐☐☐☐ Cleansing wipes or antiseptic
- ☐☐☐☐ Antibiotic cream
- ☐☐☐☐ Adhesive bandages
- ☐☐☐☐ Gauze pads
- ☐☐☐☐ Adhesive tape
- ☐☐☐☐ Butterfly closures
- ☐☐☐☐ Cotton tip applicators
- ☐☐☐☐ Tongue depressors
- ☐☐☐☐ Vinyl gloves
- ☐☐☐☐ Scissors, pair of tweezers
- ☐☐☐☐ Ice pack
- ☐☐☐☐ First aid pocket guide
- ☐☐☐☐ ....

▼ RENTING A COTTAGE

Whether you're renting a cottage or participating in a house exchange you'll want to make sure you know what you're getting into. Once you've made a list of likely destinations call the local chamber of commerce, visitors and convention bureau to get the answers to these questions.

THE TOWN

1. What's the best way to get where you're going? How far is it?
2. Will you need a car or can you use public transport or taxis?
3. What kinds of activities are there for children and teens?

THE HOUSE

1. Contact a realtor in the area.
2. Ask the chamber of commerce or visitor info centre for local rental listings.
3. Get a copy of the local newspaper.
4. Go online for rental listings.
5. Talk to several agencies and ask for photos.

THE AMENITIES

Find out if the cottage you're planning to rent has the following amenities:

- Barbeque
- Fully stocked kitchen
- Pots, pans, plates, utensils
- Patio or picnic table
- Washer and dryer
- Outdoor shower
- Television and VCR
- Recreation equipment
- Local babysitting services
- Housekeeping services
- Number of beds and sizes
- Staples — salt, pepper, spices, sugar, etc.
- ....

PACK WHATEVER IS MISSING

- ☐ Coffee filters
- ☐ Cooking oil
- ☐ Dishcloths & dish soap
- ☐ ....
- ☐ Kitchen linens
- ☐ Laundry soap
- ☐ Sheets, pillowcases
- ☐ ....
- ☐ Towels
- ☐ Food Staples — sugar salt, pepper, spices, etc.
- ☐ ....

Pack the following if you are bringing a toddler: electrical outlet covers, night light, toilet-lid latch, bathtub spout cover, doorknob covers.

▼ COTTAGE NOTES

COTTAGE	
Address	
Telephone	
Amenities	
Activities	
Notes	

COTTAGE	
Address	
Telephone	
Amenities	
Activities	
Notes	

COTTAGE	
Address	
Telephone	
Amenities	
Activities	
Notes	

Whether you're leaving on an extended vacation or just for the weekend, the following checklists will help with your packing. Use the vacation planner to organize your trip and pack the basics. Once complete, you can tear the planner sheet out and throw it into your bags — to double-check contents on the return trip. See Little Helper for additional planners. Add-on packing lists follow the planner; refer to these, depending on the type of trip and who you are bringing.

PACKING TIPS

- Use a smaller suitcase. The larger the bag, the more you'll pack in it.
- Choose wrinkle-free, natural, darker colored fabrics.
- Pack lightweight fabrics that can be hand-washed and hung to dry overnight.
- Pick mix-and-match wardrobes. Lay out clothes, check colors & discard items that don't complement each other.
- Fasten all snaps, buttons and zippers to maintain form.
- Pack footwear in separate plastic bags to avoid dents, scratches and to keep clothes clean.
- Store toiletries in small plastic containers & sealable plastic bags to prevent spills.
- Use travel-sized toiletries and bring only essential makeup.
- Call the hotel to find out if they have an iron, blow dryer, etc., that you need.
- Keep valuables to a minimum.
- Bring a small paperback or magazine and pick up other reading material along the way. Items you are going to use immediately should be packed last.

KIDS' PACKING TIPS

- Assemble outfits for the children by day. Pack each day's clothing in a separate resealable plastic bag.
- Give each child a small backpack to pack personal items such as books, crayons, games. Give each child a disposable camera and journal to create a vacation scrapbook.

VACATION PLANNER

AIRLINE Flight #	To:	Departure:	Arrival:	Cost:

ACCOMMODATIONS	Phone #	Conf. #	Cost:

CAR RENTAL	Phone #	Conf. #	Cost:

THE THINGS WE WANT TO DO ON OUR VACATION

▼ TO DO

- ☐ Schedule time off work
- ☐ Map out route, stops
- ☐ Notify schools, clubs or find sitter
- ☐ Arrange house, mail garbage and plant care
- ☐ Service the car, p. 79
- ☐ Arrange pet care
- ☐ Cancel deliveries
- ☐ Buy travelers cheques
- ☐ Buy foreign currency
- ☐ Clear credit cards
- ☐ Select clothes to pack
- ☐ Launder, mend clothes
- ☐ Shop for missing items
- ☐ Charge video batteries
- ☐ Empty fridge perishables or shop for kids groceries
- ☐ Lock house.
- ☐ ....
- ☐ ....

PACKING ESSENTIALS

TOTEBAG, PURSE OR CARRY-ON

- [ ] Wallet, purse
- [ ] Cash, credit cards
- [ ] Travellers cheques with list of numbers
- [ ] ID or driver's license
- [ ] Medical insurance cards
- [ ] Car, house keys
- [ ] Sunglasses
- [ ] ...
- [ ] ...
- [ ] Vacation planner
- [ ] Tickets, vouchers
- [ ] Maps, directions
- [ ] Watch
- [ ] Eyeglasses, repair kit
- [ ] Contact lens, solutions
- [ ] Medications
- [ ] Pictures of the kids
- [ ] ...
- [ ] ...
- [ ] Pocket knife
- [ ] Snacks, gum
- [ ] Sewing kit
- [ ] Water, juice
- [ ] Disposable wipes or damp paper towels in sealable plastic bags
- [ ] ...
- [ ] ...
- [ ] ...

TOILETRIES

- [ ] Toothbrushes, paste
- [ ] Hairbrush, accessories
- [ ] Lotions, cosmetics
- [ ] Shampoo, conditioner
- [ ] ...
- [ ] ...
- [ ] Cotton balls, swabs
- [ ] Mirror
- [ ] Manicure kit, tweezers
- [ ] Shaving supplies
- [ ] ...
- [ ] ...
- [ ] Sunscreen, lip balm
- [ ] Insect repellent
- [ ] Blow dryer
- [ ] ...
- [ ] ...
- [ ] ...

MUST HAVE

- [ ] Camera and film
- [ ] Flashlight, batteries
- [ ] Magazines, books
- [ ] Rainwear
- [ ] Small, large plastic bags for wet laundry
- [ ] Tavel first aid kit, p 79
- [ ] ...

NICE TO HAVE

- [ ] Backpack
- [ ] Night light
- [ ] Travel alarm clock
- [ ] Guidebooks
- [ ] Address book
- [ ] Stamps
- [ ] Toys, cards, games
- [ ] ...
- [ ] Video camera, tape and battery
- [ ] Radio, cd, cassette
- [ ] Headphones, batteries and music
- [ ] Extra bag for gifts
- [ ] ...
- [ ] ...

CLOTHING - BY FAMILY MEMBER

_	_	_	_	_	_	
[ ]	[ ]	[ ]	[ ]	[ ]	[ ]	Outfit for each day
[ ]	[ ]	[ ]	[ ]	[ ]	[ ]	Underwear, socks
[ ]	[ ]	[ ]	[ ]	[ ]	[ ]	Pyjamas
[ ]	[ ]	[ ]	[ ]	[ ]	[ ]	Bathing suits
[ ]	[ ]	[ ]	[ ]	[ ]	[ ]	...
[ ]	[ ]	[ ]	[ ]	[ ]	[ ]	...

_	_	_	_	_	_	
[ ]	[ ]	[ ]	[ ]	[ ]	[ ]	Caps, hats
[ ]	[ ]	[ ]	[ ]	[ ]	[ ]	Outerwear - seasonal
[ ]	[ ]	[ ]	[ ]	[ ]	[ ]	Sportswear
[ ]	[ ]	[ ]	[ ]	[ ]	[ ]	Footwear
[ ]	[ ]	[ ]	[ ]	[ ]	[ ]	...
[ ]	[ ]	[ ]	[ ]	[ ]	[ ]	...

▼ FOR SUMMER HOLIDAYS ADD

- Insect repellent
- Moleskin in case of blisters
- Ointment for insect bites
- Sun hats, caps
- Sunscreen, lip balm, zinc
- After-sun lotion
- Sunburn treatment
- Water bottles for each family member
- Worn-in walking shoes for each family member
- Rainwear
- Sportswear,equipment
- ....
- ....

AT THE BEACH

- Beach chairs
- Beachwear
- Beach towels
- Beach umbrella
- Cooler
- Cover-up
- Life jackets, waterwings,
- flotation device
- Sandals, water shoes
- Sand toys
- ....
- ....

▼ FOR WINTER HOLIDAYS ADD

- Hats
- Helmets
- Gloves/mittens
- Goggles or sunglasses
- Neck warmers
- Ski jacket and pants
- Thermal socks
- Skis, poles, boots, snowboard
- Snow boots
- Sweaters
- Turtlenecks
- Thermal underwear
- Sunscreen or lip balm
- ....
- ....
- ....

▼ LEAVING THE KIDS BEHIND

Be sure to leave the children with someone you have confidence in, someone the children like. Fill out and post the information sheets, Little Helper, p 93, 94. Remember to review them along with your emergency routines before you leave. See page 91 for other good ideas.

- cell # where you can be reached
- hotel address and phone number
- airline information
- school addresses, phone numbers
- ....
- emergency cash location
- medical cards location
- kids' schedules and contacts
- special instructions
- ....

▼ BRINGING THE KIDS

For each of your children, include the following critical medical information on an index card in your first aid kit. Throw them into your travel first aid kit before you leave on vacation

CHILD EMERGENCY INFORMATION CARD			
Name			
Birthdate			
Exact weight			
Any chronic conditions			
Any current medication, dosage			
Dates of hospitalizations			
Doctor's name and phone number			
Date of last tetanus shot			
Social security number			
Health insurance provider			
Policy number			

▼ BRINGING THE BABY

To save on packing and toting bulky baby paraphernalia, check out baby-supply rental firms. They can provide almost everything babies and toddlers need, at very reasonable rates. Baby's Away has many locations in the United States and Canada, call 1-800-571-0077. Check your hotel as well; many of them will supply some of these items so that you needn't take them with you.

- ☐☐ Acetaminophen for infants
- ☐☐ Diaper rash ointment
- ☐☐ Nasal aspirator
- ☐☐ Petroleum jelly
- ☐☐ Teething medicine
- ☐☐ Thermometer (rectal)
- ☐☐ Baby food and spoon
- ☐☐ Baby monitor
- ☐☐ Bathing supplies
- ☐☐ Bibs
- ☐☐ Blankets
- ☐☐ Bottles, nipples and caps
- ☐☐ Bottle warmer with car lighter adapter
- ☐☐ ....
- ☐☐ ....
- ☐☐ ....
- ☐☐ Car seat
- ☐☐ Child carrier, backpack, sling
- ☐☐ Collapsible stroller
- ☐☐ Diaper bag
- ☐☐ Formula and juice
- ☐☐ Pacifiers
- ☐☐ Portable crib or playpen
- ☐☐ Portable highchair or booster
- ☐☐ Waterproof sheets
- ☐☐ Childproofing kit — pack outlet covers, night light, toilet-lid latch, faucet cover and doorknob covers
- ☐☐ ....
- ☐☐ ....
- ☐☐ ....
- ☐☐ ....

▼ BRINGING THE PETS

- Health certificate
- Document of inoculations
- International permits
- Collar and ID tag
- USDA or CSA-approved carrier
- Disposable litter box
- Brush and grooming supplies
- Veterinarian's phone number
- Emergency number
- Window grills
- ....
- Leash, chain
- Muzzle
- Harness
- Towels
- Food
- Chew toys
- Treats, biscuits
- Food and water
- Bowls
- Plastic bags
- ....

▼ TRAVELING BY CAR

Traveling by car requires special consideration for a smooth enjoyable start to a family trip. Plan for many rest stops, every hour with small children and add the following items to the list of basic essentials.

- A well-packed cooler, p. 67
- Backpack for each child with favourite toys and supplies
- Pillows
- Window screens
- Activity books, magnetic travel games
- Frisbee, skipping rope or ball for playing at rest stops
- Laminated maps to mark off license plates
- ....
- Paper, washable markers
- Stickers, stamps, albums
- Lap desk or clipboard
- Tape players, headphones
- Music and books on tapes
- Gameboys, palm held games
- Video player and movies with car lighter adapter
- ....
- ....
- ....
- ....

MOM'S BAG OF TRICKS

ACTIVITY BOOKS — Miles of Smiles, I Spy, Where's Waldo?

TRAVEL GAMES — Travel Lite-Brite, Travel Magna Doodle, National Geographic Coral Reef Window Aquarium with static stick vinyl sea creatures, ready to color with markers.

STICKER BOOKS AND ALBUMS — The Most Incredible, Outrageous, Packed to the Gills, Bulging at the Seams Sticker book You've Ever seen from Klutz Inc. or make your own: glue an envelope inside a scrap book and fill with stickers. Plan on buying new ones along the way.

▼ TRAVELING ABROAD

- ☐ Passport
- ☐ Birth certificate
- ☐ Visa
- ☐ Foreign currency
- ☐ Vaccination certificate
- ☐ ....
- ☐ International driver's license
- ☐ Customs: register valuables
- ☐ International cell phone
- ☐ Voltage adapter
- ☐ ....
- ☐ Water purifying pills
- ☐ Embassy addresses
- ☐ Other addresses
- ☐ Guidebooks
- ☐ Phrase book

▼ WITH THE KIDS

BEFORE YOU GO

◆ Advise the airline that you are bringing children when you make your reservation. ◆ Request the bulkhead seat for maximum space. ◆ Ask for the travel bed if you have an infant. ◆ Reserve a child's meal for the flight ahead of time. ◆ Slings are convenient to carry baby and breast-feed discreetly. Use a backpack as your carry-on so your hands are free to hold your child. ◆ Pack surprise activities that you can pull out on the plane. See Mom's bag of tricks, p. 87 ◆ Bring extra everything — diapers, change of clothes, extra snacks, drinks. ◆ Ask each child to pack his/her own backpack with toys, crayons, stickers, books and wholesome snacks. ◆ Make sure you have a changing pad for the baby. ◆ Prepare your children with details of the trip in advance so they know what to expect on the day of the flight. ◆ Do not give your child sugary snacks, soft drinks or sugared drinks. These will only make them cranky and irritable.

PRE-FLIGHT AND BOARDING

◆ Keep your stroller with you and ask that it be treated as a carry-on. You will need it for the long walks to the plane, through the airport and for connecting flights. ◆ If you have an infant, keep your car seat with you. ◆ If you have a toddler, use a child handholder or harness. Children are free to roam and you have hands free to contend with your carry-on bag, your purse and whatever else you may need. ◆ Ask flight attendants and other boarding passengers for help, if you need it. ◆ Don't take the pre-boarding privilege offered to parents of young children. Let your children run around as long as possible to burn off excess energy.

DURING THE FLIGHT

◆ Feed baby and bring sipping cups for toddlers and chewing gum for older children during takeoff. If you or your child is congested or prone to earaches, contact your family doctor about taking medication/antihistamines before the flight. ◆ Ask for extra ice and water during drink service. ◆ Pull out your surprise entertainments one at a time as the kids get bored with what is in their own backpacks. ◆ Ask the flight attendants if they could take your kids to the cockpit when it is convenient. It's exciting for the kids and it will give you a break.

▾ PACKING FOR BUSINESS TRIPS

For your next business trip choose a large carry-on bag to avoid checking luggage, if you can. This will reduce your waiting time and solve the lost luggage problem altogether.

If you have to check some luggage, keep a change of clothes and toiletries in your carry-on in case of an emergency or lost luggage.

When choosing your travel wardrobe stick to one color scheme. Black, navy and beige work well for business. Choose pieces that you can mix and match in lightweight, cross-seasonal, natural fabrics in solid colours for your business trip.

- Identify all your luggage and slip an itinerary inside each bag.
- Carry master copies of presentation materials in your carry-on.
- Ship heavy, bulky presentation materials to your hotel in advance.
- Pack a sports watch or travel alarm if wake-up calls will be unavailable.
- When packing, iron and place each item in an individual plastic dry-cleaning bag to avoid wrinkling. Criss-cross clothing in the suitcase to reduce creases.
- Keep a dryer sheet in an open plastic bag in your suitcase to keep clothes smelling fresh. Rub it against your clothes to eliminate static cling.
- Use travel-sized toiletries and only bring essential makeup.
- Carry cosmetics in zippered transparent bags to prevent spills and for easy access.
- Wear the jewelry you will be taking.
- Hang up your clothes in a steamy bathroom with a skirt hanger clipped to the hem to pull out the creases when you arrive.

MINI FIRST AID KIT
In a resealable plastic bag:
Bandages, antibiotic cream, eye drops, cotton tip applicators, antihistamine, wet wipes, cold and pain medication, antacid and tweezers

▼ IN YOUR PURSE OR CARRY-ON

- ☐☐☐☐ Wallet, cash
- ☐☐☐☐ Credit cards
- ☐☐☐☐ ID or driver's license
- ☐☐☐☐ Passport, visa
- ☐☐☐☐ Eyeglasses, repair kit
- ☐☐☐☐ Contact lens, supplies
- ☐☐☐☐ Sunglasses
- ☐☐☐☐ Watch
- ☐☐☐☐ Medical insurance cards
- ☐☐☐☐ Prescriptions, medications
- ☐☐☐☐ Itineraries, tickets, vouchers
- ☐☐☐☐ Personal agenda
- ☐☐☐☐ Presentation materials
- ☐☐☐☐ Laptop, disks
- ☐☐☐☐
- ☐☐☐☐ ....
- ☐☐☐☐ Disposable wipes
- ☐☐☐☐ Pocket knife
- ☐☐☐☐ Recent pictures of the kids
- ☐☐☐☐ Hairbrush, ties
- ☐☐☐☐ Travel toothbrush, paste
- ☐☐☐☐ Personal feminine products
- ☐☐☐☐ Camera and film
- ☐☐☐☐ Paperback
- ☐☐☐☐ Eye shields and earplugs
- ☐☐☐☐ Mini First aid kit, p. 89

NICE TO HAVE

- ☐☐☐☐ Guidebooks and brochures
- ☐☐☐☐ Address book, paper, stamps
- ☐☐☐☐ Extra bag for souvenirs, gifts

▼ IN YOUR LUGGAGE

▼ BUSINESS WEAR

- ☐☐☐☐ Suit
- ☐☐☐☐ Skirt
- ☐☐☐☐ Pants
- ☐☐☐☐ Blazer
- ☐☐☐☐ Blouses, tops
- ☐☐☐☐ Footwear
- ☐☐☐☐ Hosiery
- ☐☐☐☐ Accessories

▼ FORMAL WEAR

- ☐☐☐☐ Outfit
- ☐☐☐☐ Footwear
- ☐☐☐☐ Hosiery
- ☐☐☐☐ Evening bag
- ☐☐☐☐ Accessories
- ☐☐☐☐ ....
- ☐☐☐☐ ....
- ☐☐☐☐ ....

▼ SPORTSWEAR

- ☐☐☐☐ Tops
- ☐☐☐☐ T-shirts
- ☐☐☐☐ Pants, jeans
- ☐☐☐☐ Jacket, cardigan
- ☐☐☐☐ Footwear
- ☐☐☐☐ Underwear, socks
- ☐☐☐☐ Pyjamas
- ☐☐☐☐ Bathing suit
- ☐☐☐☐ Exercise gear, running shoes
- ☐☐☐☐ Outerwear
- ☐☐☐☐ ....

▼ TOILETRIES

- ☐☐☐☐ Blow dryer & hair appliances (hotel may supply)
- ☐☐☐☐ Cosmetics, lotions, perfume
- ☐☐☐☐ Personal grooming supplies
- ☐☐☐☐ Manicure kit
- ☐☐☐☐ Shampoo, conditioner
- ☐☐☐☐ Shaving supplies
- ☐☐☐☐ Tweezers
- ☐☐☐☐ Mini sewing kit
- ☐☐☐☐ ....
- ☐☐☐☐ ....

BEFORE YOU GO

◆ Set up a central family calendar where members write in their activities and events. Transfer the information into your personal agenda for the time you will be away so you will know exactly when the soccer game or school play is. ◆ Pre-record some bedtime stories for your children on cassette so that they can listen to your voice before they go to sleep or hide notes in random places that your kids will find when you are away. ◆ Put up a picture of yourself (alone or with the family) on the refrigerator or in your child's bedroom. ◆ Inform your partner in advance of your travel plans. Schedule some time alone together before and after your time away. Schedule time with your children. Go on a nature hike or take in a play in your favorite park. ◆ Include your children in your travel plans. Show them where you will be on a map, the relative distance between home and there, the climate and local customs. ◆ Let them help you research information about your destination at the local library or on the Internet. ◆ Set up individual e-mail accounts for each family member to send them e-mails or e-postcards while you are away. ◆ Consider taking a child or spouse on your business trip. They'll enjoy the time away with you and seeing what you do while you are away on business. ◆ Thank your spouse and children for their support and let them know you appreciate their efforts while you're away. Once you have organized efficiently and communicated your love, enjoy your time away.

IF YOU ARE LEAVING THE CHILDREN WITH A CAREGIVER:

Pay for good help: hire someone competent and well-recommended whom the children like. If grandparents are going to fill the bill, make sure they are well supported by family and friends. Hire a teenager to help them entertain little ones after school. Plan or prepare family meals in advance and place a menu on the refrigerator. Review caregiver and emergency information, in your Little Helper, with your babysitter before you leave.

WHILE YOU ARE AWAY:

Communicate with home regularly. Call, send faxes or e-mail often.
Write letters and postcards to family and friends.
Use your trip to scout for family vacations, collecting local tourist info as you go.
Buy small gifts for your family, to let them know that you were thinking of them.

UPON YOUR RETURN:

Set aside some time for catching up with your family. Listen to everyone's news and share your traveling stories with them.

MTM'S BUSINESS TRAVEL WARDROBE

On your next business trip, consider packing only the following pieces for a mix-and-match wardrobe that will fit in one bag and serve you well on any business trip. These pieces can be combined into numerous business and casual outfits. For the ultimate travel wardrobe, pack the following:

- 1 three-piece suit
  (black, navy or beige)
  (double-breasted blazer, skirt, pants)
- 1 blouse
- 1 cardigan sweater
- 1 white T-shirt
- 1 colored T-shirt
- 1 pair of jeans
- 1 large square scarf
- 1 pair of pumps
- 1 pair of casual shoes
- Lingerie
- Sleepwear
- Toiletries

Wear the blazer, T-shirt, jeans and casual shoes on the plane. Or if you have to go to a meeting immediately when you land, switch the T-shirt and jeans for blouse and pants.

NOTES

SPECIAL PROJECTS

Why do so many people dread having to entertain, while others relish every moment of it, from the preparations to the event itself? It probably has everything to do with the planning. Preparing a dinner party for six or a fireside tête-à-tête for two is imagining everyone having a good time. Why not have fun preparing it? As our lifestyles have changed, so have the ways in which people approach entertaining. The hostess might be carpooling her children and their friends at 5 p.m. and be entertaining guests at 7! For reasons like this, it is important to begin preparations well before the first guests arrive. We hope this planner will enable you to make entertaining as pleasurable as possible for both you and your guests!

START WITH A GUEST LIST

Your guest list should be well balanced to create an interesting and animated ambience. A medley of different personalities is preferable to homogeneous characters. Once your guests have confirmed, ask if they suffer from any known food allergies.

DECIDE ON A MENU

Okay, we admit the hardest part is selecting the menu. It's so hard, actually that we went to a pro for help. Robert Bourassa is the owner and head chef of the world renown Café Henry Burger, and he has put together some menus, recipes and entertaining tips to help us along.

MAKE SURE YOU

- Have lots of food, drinks and candles.
- Set the mood by arranging cozy seating, easy lighting and good music.
- Keep a taxi phone number and acetaminophen handy for later in the evening.

ONE YOUR GUESTS ARRIVE

It is important to make your guests feel welcome, comfortable, relaxed and special. Serve drinks at the start, to break the ice and give you time for last-minute preparations. Avoid hopping back and forth to the kitchen. It's not very relaxing for your guests! It is far more enjoyable to have a genial, radiant hostess serving interesting people spaghetti and a jug of wine than having a seven-course meal served by a stressed-out hostess to boring guests.

ROMANTIC DINNER FOR TWO

A SIMPLE MENU* YOU CAN PLAN AHEAD AND HAVE READY TO GO BEFORE YOUR SPECIAL GUEST ARRIVES.

Café
Henry Burger

Roasted Mediterranean vegetable tower
with balsamic vinaigrette

❖

Grilled or pan-seared beef tenderloin on
Anna potatoes served with Bordelaise sauce
and fresh green beans

❖

Fresh strawberries Chantilly
served in a filo basket with Grand Marnier

❖

Coffee and almond tuiles

This menu can be prepared the day before for the most part with a minimum of last minute preparation, allowing you time to enjoy the evening with your guests. As an added bonus, most of the dish-washing will also be done ahead, leaving a minimum of work to do at the end of the evening. And we all know what that's like!

* This menu can be prepared for two, six, 12 or more.

ALWAYS REMEMBER TWO THINGS:

1. Plan ahead and leave yourself plenty of time for your guests.
2. Do it all with love, and you will be sure to succeed.

ROASTED MEDITERRANEAN VEGETABLE TOWER WITH BALSAMIC VINEGAR

INGREDIENTS:

- 1 small eggplant
- 1 medium zucchini
- 1 medium onion
- 1 medium ripe tomato
- 1 red pepper
- 2 Portabello mushroom caps
- 1/4 cup virgin olive oil
- 1 tsp. each of chopped: thyme, basil, rosemary, oregano; if fresh, double the quantity
- 2 Tbsp. chopped Italian parsley
- Coarse ground black pepper and coarse ground salt to taste
- 1 clove chopped fresh garlic
- small assortment of mixed lettuce (mesclun)
- vinaigrette (see proportions below)

METHOD:

- Cut all vegetables into 1/2-inch thick slices, about 2 1/2 inches in diameter. You will need one slice of each vegetable for each layer.
- Mix the oil and all herbs and spices together in a large bowl.
- Let stand for an hour
- Place all vegetables in a bowl and toss to coat well.
- In 350°F oven bake, until just slightly soft — about 10 minutes (perhaps a little more for the onion).
- Remove and let cool.
- Layer each slice of vegetable, starting with the largest on the bottom and the smallest, most colourful on top. To hold together, strip a 5-inch branch of rosemary of all leaves except those at tip; use it as a skewer, piercing the tower from the top down through the center.
- Set on a plate and refrigerate (may be kept for up to 36 hours).
- The day before, prepare the vinaigrette: blend 2 Tbsp. balsamic vinegar and 6 Tbsp. virgin olive oil, salt, pepper and 1 Tbsp. Dijon mustard.
- Before your guest arrives, place the towers on a small baking sheet and turn on the oven to 350°F.
- Place towers in the oven 10 minutes before serving.
- Place salad on the plate, place tower on the salad and drizzle with the vinaigrette.
- Serve immediately!

GRILLED OR PAN-SEARED BEEF TENDERLOIN ON ANNA POTATOES SERVED WITH BORDELAISE SAUCE AND FRESH GREEN BEANS

INGREDIENTS:

- 2 beef tenderloin about 150g each
- 2 Tbsp. oil
- Salt, crushed black pepper to taste

- 1 garlic bud, chopped
- 1 French shallot, chopped
- 1/2 cup beef sauce or gravy
- 1 cup red wine
- 2 medium potatoes, peeled
- 1/4 lb. butter, melted
- Salt, pepper
- 2 portions of fresh green beans

METHOD:

- Season and pan sear or grill the beef until slightly underdone; set aside.
- In the pan, add a little more oil and gently sauté the garlic, shallot and a good pinch of peppercorn.
- Add the wine and reduce till almost dry.
- Add beef sauce and reduce till the sauce coats the back of the spoon.
- Check the seasoning and add a dollop of butter to the sauce; set aside.
- Melt butter.
- Slice the potatoes about 1/8-inch thick, do not rinse.
- Place silicon paper on a baking sheet. Butter potato slices and place a layer of potato rounds in a circle, about 6 inches in diameter.
- Layer potato slices in these rounds, butter and season and set another layer of potatoes, season again.
- Bake in a 350°F oven for about 30 min. until golden and a bit crisp on the edges, remove and set aside.
- Blanch the green beans for 3–4 minutes until tender, cool in cold water and set aside.
- Place the beans in little bundles (2–3 bundles each) and tie together with chives, or a strip of red pepper or bacon if you wish.
- All these steps can be done in the afternoon. When you are ready to serve, place beef in a preheated 350°F oven for 6–7 minutes, add the potatoes and beans for the last 3–4 minutes.
- Gently heat the sauce in a small saucepan.
- Place the Anna potato round on each plate, place the beef on top of the potatoes and the green bean bundles around.
- Pour the sauce around the potatoes and serve.

FRESH STRAWBERRIES CHANTILLY SERVED IN A FILO BASKET WITH GRAND MARNIER

INGREDIENTS:

- 1 pint of strawberries, washed, hulled and cut in two
- 2 sheets of filo, cut in four
- 2 Tbsp. melted butter
- 2 Tbsp. Grand Marnier
- 1 Tbsp. brown sugar
- 1 cup of whipped cream

METHOD:

- Brush butter on the filo and layer 4 square pieces for each basket
- Place 2 teacups upside-down on a baking sheet and form filo baskets over the cups
- Bake at 350°F until golden; cool and set aside
- Combine the strawberries, sugar and Grand Marnier in a bowl and set aside
- When ready to serve, place a dollop of cream on the plate
- Place basket on the cream, fill with strawberry mixture and top with whipped cream.
- Finish the meal with an espresso and almond tuiles (homemade would be best).

APPETIZER

Château de Sancerre 1997
Sancerre Domaine Marnier-Lapostole, or
Fumé blanc 1998
Echo Ridge, Mendicin County
Fetzer Vineyards

Be different and offer an imported sparkling mineral water!

MAIN COURSE

Gigondas 1996
Domaine les Goubert, or
Cabernet Sauvignon 1995
Reserva, Valle del Maipo
Santa Carolina

DESSERT

Riesling Late Harvest 1995
Niagara Peninsula, or
Château des Charmes
Cordoniu Brut Classico
(sparkling wine)

"À votre Santé !" Philippe Dartois – Maître d'Hôtel et Sommelier

▾ BUFFETS

If you wish to host a larger group I suggest a buffet format, which will allow you once again, time with your guests.

- It's always good to set a theme for your buffet — such as a Provençale, Italian or Californian menu.

- Begin by choosing your main dishes (red meat, fish, poultry) and build around these. Select one main hot starch (rice, pasta, potato or other) and avoid repeating this item in other dishes such as salads. A few larger platters with cold meats or whole poached fish such as salmon are always real eye catchers.

- Add a selection of salads with an assortment of garnishes to fill in the spaces.

- Complete the menu with a few of your favourite desserts, a fruit salad, a cream dessert — and you've got to have chocolate!

- Complement your menu with the appropriate wine from the region indicated by your theme.

▾ BUFFET SUGGESTIONS

APPETIZERS AND SIDE DISHES:

- Summer mix assorted mesclun salad with balsamic vinegar & virgin olive oil vinaigrette

- Assorted condiments, and raw vegetables to add to the mesclun

- Mixed wild rice & basmati rice salad with sherry vinegar mint & peanut oil vinaigrette

- Belgian endive salad with peeled and sliced navel oranges

- Shrimp tree: take a medium size pineapple, about 60 cooked shrimps (3 per guest) and toothpicks. Place shrimp around the whole pineapple, skewered with toothpicks. Serve with seafood sauce.

- You might also consider serving sushi. I recently tried some freshly made in our local grocery store & was pleasantly surprised. The reaction will also surprise you.

LOOK AT YOUR MAIN DISH IN TWO WAYS:

1. Some meat or poultry served in a sauce with bite-size pieces which are easy to handle on your lap. It's fast, can be prepared a few days ahead and requires a minimum of last-minute attention.

2. The other choice is a focal point such as a prime rib of beef. This is always appreciated but requires a little more work. The big advantage is that if you are carving, you will have the opportunity to shine and speak to all your guests one after the other.

These dishes can be accompanied by a medley of seasonal vegetables in herb butter, and perhaps a potato gratin or even some pasta. Make sure it's short pasta, not linguini or the like. Don't try to do too many dishes; better to have fewer well prepared dishes.

- If you are daring, try a whole baked or BBQ salmon. Assume about one pound for every four to five guests. Cook about 10 minutes per pound, wrapped in strong aluminum foil in a medium BBQ with lots of butter and herbs.

AND FOR DESSERT:

- As for dessert, three selections is more than enough. Make sure they are distinctive and varied in flavour. Fresh fruit salad is a must. Perhaps a silky chocolate mousse and a rich cheesecake, or something in puff pastry. Keep the portions small so your guests can try them all.

HOW MUCH TO MAKE:

Determining how much to make is always difficult, even for me. Plan on an average portion of meat or fish for each guest. When it comes to all the rest, make about 1/3 of a normal portion of each dish and you will have plenty.

My best advice is to take the time to enjoy what you're doing. Have fun with it and don't worry about following recipes exactly. Cooking is more of an art than a science, so go with the flow. You may surprise yourself and your guests.

Enjoy,
Robert

TO DO LIST!

▼ A WEEK BEFORE

- [ ] Fill out entertaining planner
- [ ] Buy non-perishables
- [ ] Buy beer, wine and alcohol
- [ ] Thoroughly clean your home
- [ ] ....
- [ ] ....

▼ 3-4 DAYS BEFORE

- [ ] Prepare and freeze dessert or other menu items
- [ ] Clean, iron tablecloth, napkins
- [ ] Clean your cutlery
- [ ] Grocery shopping
- [ ] Check your serving equipment; borrow what you are missing
- [ ] ....
- [ ] ....

THE DAY BEFORE

- [ ] Pick up and arrangefresh flowers
- [ ] Wash and dry lettuceand crudités; Store in refrigerator in plastic bags
- [ ] Prepare butter and put in dishes
- [ ] Prepare your vinaigrette and sauces
- [ ] Clean glasswear
- [ ] Prepare dessert (if not frozen)
- [ ] Have the children clean their rooms
- [ ] ....
- [ ] ....

THE DAY OF THE PARTY

A.M.

- [ ] Tidy up the house
- [ ] - clean the bathroom
- [ ] - put out clean hand towels
- [ ] - change toilet paper
- [ ] - set out acetaminophen
- [ ] Empty the dishwasher
- [ ] Sink should be spotless
- [ ] Unclutter counters
- [ ] Clear hall closet for coats
- [ ] ....
- [ ] ....
- [ ] ....

P.M.

- [ ] Prepare your main dish
- [ ] Thaw dessert if frozen
- [ ] Set the table
- [ ] Lay out coffee and tea

ONE HOUR BEFORE

- [ ] Ask someone to walk dog
- [ ] Take a bath or shower
- [ ] Get dressed, relax - have a glass of wine!
- [ ] ....
- [ ] ....

▼ ENTERTAINMENT PLANNER

EVENT			
DATE		TIME	
LOCATION		# OF GUESTS	

MENU

RECIPE	WHERE'S THE RECIPE?

SHOPPING LIST

INGREDIENTS AND OTHERS:

CHRISTMAS

Ho Ho Ho Merry Christmas! We all look forward to this special time of year; a time to share with loved ones and enjoy a rest from work and school. To make your Christmas more joyful and less stressful keep the following in mind as you make your holiday plans.

The "I shoulds" and "I have tos" — along with stretching the family budget are the major sources of stress over the holidays.

- Eliminate activities that you do only because you feel you should.
- Schedule lots of time for rest, your spouse and your children.
- Keep the kids to their daily routine as much as possible throughout the season.
- Set a holiday spending limit and stick to it.

▼ TRADITIONS

Christmas traditions can be as simple as making a special desert or as elaborate as hosting a yearly tree-trimming party. Much of the joy of Christmas is looking forward to and remembering the things that happen only at Christmas. traditions can be passed down through generations or created anew when we start our own families.

OUR CHRISTMAS TRADITIONS	NEW IDEAS

Once you have worked your way through this section and have scheduled your activities and to-dos, post them in your More Time Moms Family Organizer for all to see and share in the excitement and anticipation of a joyous Christmas season.

▼ CHRISTMAS FUN

Christmas is a time for doing special things with the family, but the holiday events can fill up the calendar all too quickly. We often find ourselves running from one event to the next without so much as a breath in between. To enjoy a merry time and reduce holiday stress, prioritize important and fun family time.

- Together as a family, list the fun things you want to do
- Decide on a realistic number of events for the holiday period.
- Eliminate unrealistic and unaffordable choices.
- Schedule the rest.

You can have great fun and create family traditions around these simple things.

- [ ] Getting the Christmas tree
- [ ] Trimming the tree
- [ ] Santa Claus parade
- [ ] Toy store tour
- [ ] Evening neighborhood tour of Christmas lights
- [ ] Visit Santa
- [ ] Caroling
- [ ] Midnight mass on Christmas Eve
- [ ] Sleigh ride
- [ ] School and church bazaars
- [ ] Volunteering at shelters
- [ ] Building a snowman/snow angels
- [ ] Skating
- [ ] Tobogganing
- [ ] Skiing
- [ ] Watch a favorite seasonal movies
- [ ] Checking your newspaper for local Christmas events
- [ ] ....

Make a list of the things you usually do at Christmas and the things you feel you have to do. Go through this list very carefully. Ask yourself these two important questions: Did I enjoy this event? Was it important to be there for others? If the answer is yes, schedule it in. If not, eliminate it from your schedule.

FUN THINGS TO DO OVER THE HOLIDAYS

ACTIVITY	DATE	TIME

CHRISTMAS COUNTDOWN

BY DECEMBER 1ST

- [ ] Check outdoor Christmas lights and replace bulbs or strings.
- [ ] Hang Christmas lights.
- [ ] Collect pine cones to mix with Christmas balls for a basket display.
- [ ] Get grapevines for wreaths.
- [ ] Pick up decorations for wreaths.
- [ ] Purchase candy/small gifts for Advent calendars.
- [ ] ....
- [ ] ....
- [ ] ....
- [ ] ....

1ST WEEK OF DECEMBER

- [ ] Plan holiday entertaining.
- [ ] Put out Advent calendar(s).
- [ ] Hang door decorations.
- [ ] Turn on outside lights.
- [ ] Put up artificial tree (if used).
- [ ] Replace everyday knickknacks with Christmas decor.
- [ ] Christmas baking to be frozen.
- [ ] Send distant Christmas cards and packages.
- [ ] ....
- [ ] ....
- [ ] ....
- [ ] ....

2ND WEEK OF DECEMBER

- [ ] Send Christmas cards.
- [ ] Check Christmas tree lights and replace bulbs or strings.
- [ ] Get tree.
- [ ] Make evergreen garlands.
- [ ] Decorate front entrance.
- [ ] Decorate window boxes.
- [ ] Decorate inside stair railings.
- [ ] Decorate tree a few days before your first entertaining engagement.
- [ ] Grocery shopping for non-perishables and beverages.
- [ ] ....
- [ ] ....
- [ ] ....
- [ ] ....

3RD WEEK OF DECEMBER

- [ ] Complete all decorations and stop to enjoy them.
- [ ] Finish last-minute Christmas shopping.
- [ ] Wrap presents.
- [ ] Grocery shopping for Christmas dinner.
- [ ] Bake fresh goods.
- [ ] ....
- [ ] ....
- [ ] ....
- [ ] ....

▾ CHRISTMAS CARDS

Christmas cards seem to be a thing of the past, but they are still a nice way to stay in touch with people you don't see on a regular basis. With a little effort and planning, they can be done in a snap.

- While watching TV one night in November, sign and address your cards. You don't have to mail them until December.
- If you like to write a little note in them, start earlier — around the second week of November.
- Have one of the children input addresses on the computer to create a perpetual list, and print out envelopes. This could be a job to help them earn their own Christmas money.
- Keep the Christmas cards you receive to check against your list and add anyone you have forgotten, for next year.
- Fill your cards with Christmas confetti and have a good laugh as you seal the envelopes thinking of all the confetti falling out when recipients open them up.
- Recycle Christmas cards by using them the following year for gift tags on your presents.

▾ DECORATING

Schedule your decorating, by the week or weekend, with a start and finish date so you can gradually work up to a completely decorated house.

DECORATING IDEAS

▼ BAKING

Christmas baking can be an overwhelming chore. If you don't like to bake, don't feel obligated to do it. There are so many good bazaar and store-bought desserts out there; you needn't feel like you have missed a thing! If you think you will miss the smell of Christmas baking, add cinnamon, cloves and orange peel to water and let simmer on the stove — or buy a frozen uncooked pie and bake it just before guests arrive.

If you are going to bake, start baking early since most things can be frozen. That way, you will always have something prepared to welcome unexpected guests. Try to pick a day when the kids can bake. They really love cutting and decorating. Sugar cookies or gingerbread men are the simplest recipes. Decorate with sparkles and chocolate chips before baking, so that all the mess can be cleaned up at once. Organize a cookie exchange with other mothers who bake. You save time and money baking large quantities of one thing and exchanging with other moms, so your pantry is filled with a variety of delicious Christmas baking. A box of your favorite baked goods is always a great gift for neighbors and party hostesses.

CHRISTMAS BAKING

RECIPE	WHERE'S THE RECIPE?

INGREDIENTS TO PICK UP

▼ GIFTS

Christmas gifts needn't be elaborate. Often the smallest, least expensive gift is the perfect gift because you know it will mean the most to the receiver.

- An easy way to choose a gift for someone is to get something that relates to his or her interests. Listen closely to your loved ones, friends and co-workers for clues to their passions.
- If you have a large family pick names from a hat. Thanksgiving is a convenient time to do this when everyone is together.
- Set a budget and stick to it. Ask your kids and spouse, "What is the one thing you really want?" Get it if you can.
- Take the opportunity to teach your children the joys of giving to the community and spreading Christmas spirit. Sit down with the family to determine your community and charitable donations this year.
- Homemade gifts are always well received, but they do take time, so don't leave them to the last minute.
- Catalogs and on-line stores offer unique gifts that can save you time.
- Gift wrap presents as you go and store them at your neighbour's place, so the kids can't peek. You can store your neighbour's presents in return.
- Start saving the comics from the newspaper to use as Christmas wrapping.

GIFT IDEAS

- Gift certificates to movies or movie rentals (include microwave popcorn and their favorite seasoned salt).
- Prepaid calling card in a new wallet, for teens.
- Package up lots of small gifts in a nice keepsake box, for kids.
- Potted plants arranged in a nice basket to chase away winter blues.
- A couple of nice mugs with some flavored hot chocolate.
- An ornament as a keepsake for each family member.

CHRISTMAS GIFT LIST

NAME	INTERESTS	GIFT	WRAPPED

▾ ENTERTAINING

Holiday entertaining can be whatever you want it to be. You can go all out with a full course meal or just have family and friends for a potluck supper.

A full course meal takes planning. Use one of the entertainment planners in Little helper to help you along. Make sure you have the kids organized if they are not involved in the dinner, so that they will be content to leave you alone with your guests.

Potluck suppers can be as much fun as a formal dinner. Everyone can bring their favorite meal and it can be served as a sit down meal or a buffet. Decide what best suits your crowd. Ask each person to bring copies of their recipe to share with the guests. People are generally willing to bring whatever you want — main dish, dessert or a salad.

Progressive Parties are fun too. Each family serves one course of the meal. The party begins at the home of whoever is serving the hors d'œuvres and pre-dinner drinks. It then moves to the next home for the first course, then on to the next for the main meal, and so on till you end up at the last home for after dinner drinks. Quite often the person with the capacity to seat the most has the main course, and the ones with the youngest kids serve after-dinner drinks so the kids can be put to bed at a reasonable hour. This does not have to be anything fancy, and is usually a good time for everyone.

ENTERTAINING I WOULD LIKE TO DO THIS YEAR

▾ CHRISTMAS DINNER

Sit down with your family to plan Christmas dinner, to best suit your needs. If your children are small and you are looking for a break, serve somthing simple like hot turkey sandwiches and french fries. If you traditionally serve an 8 course meal to a large group, get help or turn your Christmas dinner into a pot luck. Once you plan your menu, be sure to make a detailed shopping list so that you are not running back and forth to the grocery store during the last few days before Christmas.

DINNER PLANS

MENU	WHERE'S THE RECIPE?

GROCERIES

If you traditionally go out for Christmas Dinner, but find yourself torn between families, ask one of them to move their Christmas dinner to the 24th or 26th so that you see everyone, every year.

CONSIDER THIS BEFORE YOU BEGIN

- Involve your child in the party planning process. It is the most exciting day of the year for him/her and the more involved in the preparations he/she is are the happier he/she will be. Ask your child to help pick a theme, choose a birthday cake, fill the loot bags and make the invitations.

- Pick a theme for your child's party based on your child's likes and interests. You can include music, food, colors, decorations and games in your theme. It does not have to be expensive, and almost anything can be homemade.

- Before setting the date, time and duration of your party, check school calendars and take into consideration naps, extracurricular activities & your child's best time of day.

- Prepare your child for the birthday party by telling him what is going to happen, how to greet guests and how to thank guests for their gifts.

- When the children are little, have small presents or loot bags set aside for siblings to open at the end while the birthday child is enjoying his gifts — and keep an extra one of everything, just in case.

- Keep the party short, between one and two hours, and lay out the running order,

- Keep the party rolling so the children don't act up. Start by giving early arrivals something quiet to do such as crafts like making hats, masks or loot bags.

- Rent a video in case the games run out or parents are late picking up their children. If you're planning an outdoor party, set up a spot in case of rain.

- Serve non-messy nibbles first — pretzels, chips, crackers, corn chips. Choose finger foods, little sandwiches, veggies and dip for tiny hands. Save the gooey stuff like pizza and cake for the end.

- Designate a party room or area to contain the mess and supervise the guests.

- Good sources for party info are the library and the Internet. You can start with a visit to www.birthdaypartyideas.com and, for a Canadian supplier that delivers to your door, visit www.thebirthdayzoneplus.com.

CRITICAL PATH

2 OR 3 WEEKS BEFORE

- [ ] Fill out your planner
- [ ] Book special props, costumes
- [ ] Make costumes
- [ ] Buy or make non-perishable food and party supplies
- [ ] Send out invitations
- [ ] ....

A WEEK BEFORE

- [ ] Confirm guest list - call parents
- [ ] Confirm special bookings
- [ ] Enrol and delegate tasks to helpers — food, games, etc.
- [ ] Set aside music, videos for party
- [ ] Check cameras, flash, batteries
- [ ] Shop for party food, film, etc.
- [ ] Order or bake birthday cake if baking, freeze it unfrosted
- [ ] Prepare foods to be frozen
- [ ] ....
- [ ] ....

THE DAY BEFORE

- [ ] Defrost & decorate cake
- [ ] Get craft supplies organized
- [ ] Prepare games, wrap prizes
- [ ] Fill loot bags
- [ ] Clean & childproof party area
- [ ] Set up rooms and furniture
- [ ] Put up non-perishable decorations
- [ ] Prepare party food recipes
- [ ] Recharge video camera
- [ ] Decorate room
- [ ] Hide toys child won't share
- [ ] Prepare birthday child's clothes
- [ ] Lay out family outfits
- [ ] ....
- [ ] ....
- [ ] ....

THE DAY OF...

- [ ] Pick up or frost birthday cake
- [ ] Inflate balloons
- [ ] Defrost prepared food
- [ ] Prepare food & drinks
- [ ] Set and decorate the table
- [ ] Set out non-perishable foods
- [ ] Put pets in a safe area
- [ ] ....
- [ ] ....

LEAVE AMPLE TIME TO DRESS YOUR CHILD, YOURSELF AND OTHER FAMILY MEMBERS FOR THE PARTY.

SEE LITTLE HELPER FOR MORE PARTY PLANNERS

▼ BIRTHDAY PARTY PLANNER

Date:		Place:
Time:	From:	To:
THEME		
Colours:		

ACTIVITY SCHEDULE		DURATION
Music:		

FOOD	

▼ PARTY SUPPLIES:

- ☐ Invitations
- ☐ Thank-you notes
- ☐ Balloons
- ☐ Streamers
- ☐ Banners
- ☐ Wall decorations
- ☐ ....
- ☐ Door decorations
- ☐ Lawn ornaments
- ☐ Masks
- ☐ Hats
- ☐ Costumes
- ☐ Game props
- ☐ ....
- ☐ Loot bags
- ☐ Pinata
- ☐ Centrepiece
- ☐ Napkins
- ☐ Dinner plates
- ☐ Dessert plates
- ☐ ....
- ☐ Cups
- ☐ Utensils
- ☐ Straws
- ☐ Candles, sparklers
- ☐ Craft supplies
- ☐ ....
- ☐ ....

THEME-RELATED PARTY GAMES

The following party games can be easily adapted to almost any theme. For example: Barbie and Construction themes

Bucket toss: You can toss anything into anything - Barbie clothes into a suitcase or construction tools into a toolbox.

Dress up relay race: Divide children into two teams. Have a child from each team run from one end of the room to the other and put on a gown, gloves, hat and heels or T-shirt, flannel work shirt, work boots, tool belt and hard hat. Once dressed, the child must take it all off and the next child puts it on. The first team to complete wins.

Guessing games: Guess the number of beads in the jewelry box. Guess the number of nails in the tool chest.

Guess the character: Each guest has a sticker of a character on his/her back and gets to ask five questions of the other guests in order to guess who they are. Use Barbie's friends — Skipper, Ken and all the special Barbies. Use different construction vehicles.

Musical chairs: Substitute pink pillows or cardboard manhole covers and play theme-related music like Miss America or Working On The Railroad.

Memory games: Put several theme-related items on a tray. Guests have 30 seconds to memorize the item. Take the tray away and have them write down as many items as they can remember.

Hot potato: Play theme-related music and pass the Barbie doll or the construction hat.

Pass the parcel: Play theme-related music and pass a parcel wrapped in layers of pink paper for Barbie and yellow and black for the construction theme. When the music stops the guest is allowed to unwrap one layer, till they get to the prize in the center. Make sure each layer contains a small candy or treat.

Pin the tail on: Put the high heel shoe or the hat on Barbie, or put the bucket shovel on the bulldozer.

Ring toss: Toss the ring around any theme-related item. Use Barbie or a toy construction crane.

Simon says: Change it to "Barbie says" or "Foreman says."

Treasure hunt: Use Barbie articles or construction items, small toys, pencils, stickers, puzzle pieces, anything that ties in with your theme.

BIRTHDAY NOTES

PLANNING YOUR GARDEN

Do you dream of a beautiful, lush, almost carefree garden? If yes, read the following principles on planning, shopping and caring for your garden. They will save you time and money by helping you select the right plant for the right place.

▼ THE PURPOSE OF THIS GARDENING PROJECT

What do you want to accomplish with your garden, now and in the future? Every plant, and group of plants can fulfil a specific purpose that will structure an enjoyable outdoor space. Start by determining what you want to accomplish with your outdoor spaces.

Here are some possibilities:

- ☐ Visual screen
- ☐ Segregate outdoor spaces
- ☐ Control circulation
- ☐ Provide shade
- ☐ Prevent erosion
- ☐ ....
- ☐ ....
- ☐ Attract birds, butterflies
- ☐ Attract aquatic fauna
- ☐ Grow fruits, vegetables
- ☐ For sounds - rustling leaves, water
- ☐ Easy to maintain
- ☐ ....
- ☐ ....

▼ KNOW YOUR SITE

Elements like sunlight, exposure and soil have a definite impact on your plants. Observe your surroundings and make note of the characteristics of your garden site

- ☐ Sunny
- ☐ Shady
- ☐ Partially sunny, a.m. or p.m.
- ☐ Windy
- ☐ Protected from harsh winter winds from northwest
- ☐ Southern exposure — dry and hot
- ☐ Northern exposure — shady and cool
- ☐ Eastern exposure — strong a.m. sun
- ☐ Western exposure — declining heat and sunlight

▼ MICROCLIMACTIC ELEMENTS

- ☐ Wall — protected from winter winds
- ☐ Large body of water nearby
- ☐ Trees protecting from harsh weather
- ☐ Tree roots competing for nutrients and moisture
- ☐ Corridor of wind
- ☐ ....
- ☐ ....
- ☐ ....
- ☐ ....

▼ KNOW YOUR SOIL

Soil supports plants and provides food and water to help them grow. The nature of your soil impacts the health and look of your garden.

▼ EVALUATE SOIL STRUCTURE

- ☐ Loose — good drainage and easy growth for root system
- ☐ Compacted, hard surface — prevents oxygen and water penetration
- ☐ Poorly drained — water puddles or boggy soil
- ☐ Poor water retention - often sandy, soil dries out quickly

▼ EVALUATE SOIL COMPOSITON

- ☐ Rich — dark organic matter full of worms and insects
- ☐ Fertile — contains minerals such as nitrogen, phosphorus, potassium and other trace elements
- ☐ Soil pH — scale 1 to 10, from very acid (0) to very alkaline (10). Most plants do better in a moderate pH of 6 or 7; you can buy test strips at your local nursery

SOIL TEST:

To test the structure of your soil, simply throw a handful of topsoil into a glass jar filled with water. Shake it, then let it settle. The big particles of sand and rock will sink to the bottom and the organic matter will float to the surface. Healthy soil contains a minimum of 5% organic matter. A laboratory test is required to determine exact nutrient content. Most problems with soil structure and composition can be corrected with composting. See the section "Care for your garden" for tips on how to make compost.

▼ CHOOSE YOUR PLANTS

It is very important to consider the results of your site and soil observations when selecting your plant material. Some plants will thrive in specific soil conditions (like irises in boggy soil or lupines in sandy soil). Choose plants that will thrive in your soil conditions. Choose species and varieties resistant to disease and pests. Don't yield to temptation, select only the plants that fulfill the purpose of your garden project.

CHARACTERISTICS OF PLANT MATERIAL REQUIRED FOR THIS PROJECT:

- height
- width
- colour of foliage
- colour of flowers
- blooming period
- propagation method — clumps, seeds, roots
- texture
- smell
- growth speed
- cost

▼ MY GARDEN PLAN

▼ SHOPPING FOR THIS PROJECT

Now that you have a vision of what you want to create, you're ready to take action. Prepare a list of everything you'll need before you go shopping. Purchase tools best suited to your size and strength.

TOOLS

- [ ] digging spade
- [ ] digging fork
- [ ] rake
- [ ] hose - long enough to reach to the farthest corner of your garden
- [ ] hoe
- [ ] hand fork
- [ ] cultivator
- [ ] pruning shears

PLANTS

▼ ANNUALS, PERENNIALS, TREES, SHRUBS:

AND

▼ SOIL. FERTILIZER, MULCH, COMPOST, ETC.

▾ CARING FOR YOUR GARDEN

Your garden will thrive if you carefully select suitable plants and if your soil is rich in nutrients. Use compost, mulch and fertilizer to build healthy soil.

COMPOST

Compost is the result of well-decomposed organic material. It provides your plants with nutrients and increases their resistance to disease and pests. It is dark, almost black, light, loose and odorless.

COMPOST BINS:

Choose a sunny to partially sunny, well-drained, out-of-the-way corner in your garden for your compost bin. Heat accelerates the process of decomposition. A bin secures the environment inside the compost pile, like the water content and heat level. You can purchase compost bins at your local garden center or ask city hall if they provide them at a discount.

To make your own compost bin, consider the following tips.

- Make sure it is well aerated with holes. A good wire mesh is an easy way to make an efficient compost bin. Simply shape the mesh into a vertical cylinder, closing it with wire.
- Place your pile directly on healthy ground. Micro-organisms need direct access to the compost to start the process of decomposition.
- Consider how you'll empty your bin once your compost is mature. It should be easy to get the organic matter in and out of the bin.
- Protect your pile from rain. Nutrients will leach with excessive water.

HOW TO MAKE A COMPOST PILE:

- Add organic elements, in layers, alternating with a few shovelfuls of top-soil from a corner of your garden to begin the process of decomposition. Do this consistently over several weeks until you have a heap of about three cubic feet. Let this first pile decay completely and start another one beside it.
- If it smells bad, aerate the pile with a garden fork or turn it with a shovel. Make sure the water drains well at the bottom.
- Never use meat, bones, grease or dairy products in the compost pile; they attract rodents. Always cover kitchen garbage with soil or bury it in the compost pile.
- Do not use exotic fruits, such as bananas and citrus fruits in northern climes. They do not decay properly in these soils.

COMPOSTING:

Let your compost sit between one to three months before using. To shorten the decay time by half, shred everything into one-inch bits. If you're in a hurry, put your kitchen waste in a blender with water. Pour the solution into a hole in the center of the compost pile. This keeps the pile moist and makes nutrients readily available to micro-organisms.

- Your pile is mature once it turns almost black, has a fresh smell of forest ground and is loose. If you find big fat worms and small insects, you're on your way to having a lush garden.
- You can prepare compost tea by diluting some of the organic matter in water and pouring it around your plants.

MULCHING

Mulching is simply covering your garden beds with a layer of organic or inorganic material. Many consider mulch to be the gardener's best friend as it:

- Conserves soil moisture; may reduce watering as much as 50%!
- Helps plants survive draughts
- Controls weeds
- Prevents soil compaction; provides easy infiltration of water and oxygen; keeps the soil loose and facilitates weeding
- Fights disease: prevents the carrying of fungus from plant to plant
- Protects root systems: prevents erosion and rapid water runoff

Consider cost and availability when choosing your mulch.

- Compost: fertilizes plants and warms up soil.
- Grass cuttings: rich in nitrogen, lay in thin layers.
- Chopped leaves: mown leaves keep the ground cool in summer.
- Old sawdust: aged at least one year.
- Peat moss: attractive, inexpensive but may dry out your soil in summer.
- Pine needles: very effective on weeds, too acidic for neutral soil plants.
- Seaweed: less attractive but very fertile.
- Shredded bark, wood chips: attractive and effective.
- River pebbles or stones: very attractive, gradually release midday sun.
- Geotextile: synthetic fabric that lets water and air in and out of the soil; will last for years but must be covered with more attractive mulch.

FERTILIZING

Finally, you may want to boost your plants with fertilizer. A word of caution however: fertilizers cannot replace the conditions necessary for a healthy garden. Over-fertilizing will harm your plants. Fertilizers are vitamins, not main meals. Fertilizers provide one or more of three primary nutrients:

Nitrogen — provides lush, green foliage and rapid growth to plants.
- Too much: plants are vulnerable to disease
- Too little: slows plant growth
- Signs: small yellow leaves, small plants

Phosphorus — strengthens plant stems, increases resistance to pests and diseases, builds healthy root systems and fosters fruit and flower development. Always add phosphorus when transplanting.
- Too much: blocks out the absorbtion of other nutrients and minerals
- Too little: plant does not produce flower or fruit
- Signs: reddish purple leaves, no flowers or fruit

Potassium — manufactures starch, sugars and proteins in plants; builds strong root systems and boosts immune systems, making plants more resistant to cold, windy winters.
- Too much: slows plant growth
- Too little: misshapen flowers
- Signs: small plants, misshapen flowers

You can buy fertilizer in different strengths and forms, or you can use organic fertilizers.

ORGANIC FERTILIZERS	APPLICATION	NITROGEN	PHOSPHOROUS	POTASSIUM
Manure aged/dried	Yearly	✔	✔	
Compost	Yearly	✔		
Blood meal	Yearly	✔		
Rock phosphate	Yearly		✔	
Granite dust	Fall			✔
Cow manure	Fall			✔
Manure tea	Weekly	✔		
Fish emulsion (5-1-1)	Weekly	✔		

A GARDENER'S AGENDA

The actual month you undertake each task may vary according to your location in North America, but this agenda is seasonally correct for all North American climates.

FEBRUARY

- [ ] Plan your garden
- [ ] Place catalog orders for new garden tools and seeds
- [ ] Start seedlings indoors
- [ ] Gently shake excess snow from shrubs and trees

APRIL OR WHEN GROUND THAWS

- [ ] Remove protection from shrubs
- [ ] Treat fruit trees, shrubs with dormant oil
- [ ] Prune fruit and crabapple trees
- [ ] Remove dead branches from trees and shrubs

MAY

- [ ] Aerate lawn
- [ ] Rake grass
- [ ] Start new compost pile
- [ ] Aerate and water compost pile
- [ ] Plant perennials
- [ ] Transplant or divide mature clumps of perennials; add a transplanting solution, rich in phosphorus
- [ ] Plant tender summer bulbs
- [ ] Spread annual and perennial grass seed
- [ ] Spread nitrogen-rich fertilizer into borders and lawn
- [ ] Spread a 1-inch layer of compost on flowers and shrub borders
- [ ] Prepare vegetable garden beds
- [ ] Clean water basin for pond

EARLY JUNE

- [ ] Add topsoil to lawn
- [ ] Acclimate seedlings gradually to outdoor light and temperature
- [ ] Seed annuals in vegetable garden
- [ ] Transplant seedlings outdoors
- [ ] Plant annuals and aquatic plants
- [ ] Aerate and water compost pile
- [ ] Keep all grass clippings and other organic material for compost pile
- [ ] Add phosphorus-rich fertilizer to flowering plants in containers
- [ ] Inspect plants for pests and disease
- [ ] Mow and water lawn regularly
- [ ] Water and weed gardens regularly

LATE JUNE

- [ ] Prune flowering shrubs and perennials after blooming period
- [ ] Discard or compost brown tulip stems and foliage
- [ ] Trim evergreens at the end of growth spurt
- [ ] ....
- [ ] ....
- [ ] Spray foliage of ornamental plants with fish emulsion
- [ ] Inspect plants for pests and disease
- [ ] Aerate and water compost pile
- [ ] Mow and water lawn regularly
- [ ] Water and weed gardens regularly
- [ ] ....
- [ ] ....

JULY AND AUGUST

- [ ] Take the time to smell the flowers
- [ ] Spray foliage of ornamental plants with fish emulsion
- [ ] Prune flowering shrubs and perennials after blooming period
- [ ] ....
- [ ] Prune birches and maples
- [ ] Inspect plants for pests and disease
- [ ] Aerate and water compost pile
- [ ] Weed and water when necessary
- [ ] Mow lawn as needed
- [ ] ....

SEPTEMBER

- [ ] Divide overgrown perennials
- [ ] Prune trees
- [ ] Apply granular fertilizer rich in potassium
- [ ] ....
- [ ] Weed where necessary
- [ ] Spread compost in 1-inch layer in plant beds
- [ ] Start new compost pile
- [ ] Mow lawn as needed

OCTOBER

- [ ] Compost or discard dead annuals
- [ ] Replace summer annuals with asters or chrysanthemums
- [ ] Plant spring bulbs
- [ ] Remove, store tender summer bulbs
- [ ] Rake leaves
- [ ] ....
- [ ] Water evergreens generously
- [ ] Compost remnants of veggie garden
- [ ] Empty and clean pond
- [ ] Empty and store flower containers
- [ ] Add mulch to plant beds
- [ ] Install bird feeders
- [ ] ....

NOVEMBER

- [ ] Cover shrubs sensitive to winter winds
- [ ] Post flags along borders for snow plow

DECEMBER

- [ ] Gardener's Holiday. Merry Christmas!

Wills. Well, that's something many of us haven't taken care of yet and mostly because the process seems difficult and expensive. Not so — and the simple fact is that if you have minor-aged children, you need a will.

WHY DO I NEED A WILL?

- To appoint a guardian for your children. A will clearly states whom you would like to bring up your children. It is the best way to ensure that what you want for your children comes to pass and eliminates disagreement among family members as to your wishes.

- To appoint a trustee. This will ensure that someone you trust will manage your money and property until the children reach the age at which you deem them capable of handling their own assets.

- To control the distribution of your property. Without a will, your provincial, territorial or state governments determine the distribution of your assets and it is not always as you might assume or might like. Did you know that in some provinces, for instance, if you die intestate your assets do not go to your spouse but directly to your children? Without a will, your survivors' well being is not assured.

- To save estate taxes. Properly written wills can lead to substantial tax savings, ensuring that the bulk of your estate is handed down to your survivors.

- To avoid family disputes. It is a sad thing to watch family members argue over the division of an estate.

HOW DO I DRAW UP MY WILL?

- Handwritten will: This type of will is not valid in most provinces and states.

- Do-it-yourself packages: These packages can produce adequate results; unfortunately, they do not always address particular circumstances, nor do they consider better options. They can prove valuable as educational tools but are not a substitute for professional guidance and may not be valid when you move.

- Hire a lawyer: A lawyer can prepare a will that is valid anywhere, provides for your particular situation and is tax protected. Legal fees for wills are proportionate to the complexity of the situation. If your situation is simple, your fees will be minimal, and if complicated, there is an endless list of problems and pitfalls a lawyer can help avoid.

APPOINTMENTS

Before you draw up your will, take some time to think about your estate appointments. Each of these helpers will be taking on a great responsibility and it is important to make sure that they are up to the task and well informed of their duties.

- Legal guardian ....
- Trustee ....
- Executor(s) ....

EXECUTOR'S DUTIES

It is important that you select an executor — or even a couple of executors — because the duties of the executors will be onerous. Upon your death, it will be their duty to:

- Locate your financial and legal paperwork
- Notify banks, investment brokers and creditors of your death
- Arrange for a bond, if necessary
- File claims for insurance, pensions and other death benefits
- Collect all moneys owed the estate, including paychecks
- Obtain court authority to pay interim support to beneficiaries and to pay off estate debts
- File deceased's final income tax papers
- Evaluate and settle claims against the estate
- Defend any lawsuits against the estate
- File succession duty returns
- Apportion and collect death duties from beneficiaries
- Distribute the estate

EXECUTOR'S FILES

Now that you understand what you are asking your executor to undertake, you will want to make his/her job as easy as possible. Build a file for your executor, keep it with your will and let your executor know where all is kept. This file should contain the location of everything that your executor will need to do his job. Be sure to include contact numbers for beneficiaries, representatives and institutions in the file.

- ☐ Personal: ID, passports, birth certificates, social insurance number, etc.
- ☐ Financial assets: Bank accounts, RRSPs, RESPs, deeds, etc.
- ☐ Material assets: Home inventory, assets elsewhere.
- ☐ Income sources: Job, pension, investments, etc.
- ☐ Debts: Loans, mortgages, credit cards, bills to pay, etc.
- ☐ Other: Safety deposit key, safe key, tax returns, etc.

LIVING WILLS describe your wishes about any life prolonging medical procedures that could be used in case of serious injury or medical illness. You may want to draw one up to minimize family turmoil, should the need for one arise.

NOTES